The Candle Store

The Candle Store

Mary Greer

Columbus, Ohio

The views and opinions expressed in this book are solely those of the author and do not reflect the views or opinions of Gatekeeper Press. Gatekeeper Press is not to be held responsible for and expressly disclaims responsibility of the content herein.

The Candle Store

Published by Gatekeeper Press
2167 Stringtown Rd, Suite 109
Columbus, OH 43123-2989
www.GatekeeperPress.com

Copyright © 2021 by Mary Greer
All rights reserved. Neither this book, nor any parts within it may be sold or reproduced in any form or by any electronic or mechanical means, including information storage and retrieval systems, without permission in writing from the author. The only exception is by a reviewer, who may quote short excerpts in a review.

Library of Congress Control Number: 2021939325

ISBN (paperback): 9781662914591
eISBN: 9781662914607

For DAE, of course

PROLOGUE

"The Candle Store," by Michelle Jackson
circa 1995

On her way to the candle store
To find religion inside
Having aged a lifetime to find
High derision outside

Dark extremes turn pale today
By the vision of light
Shining flames that light the way
Eternal crystal inside

Once inside, she inhales the candles
Enchanted fire divine
Dancing flames, reflection of light
Like a vision entwined

Silent dreams, she sails away
In light, no need to hide
Breathless flight, no words to say
The candles now flicker inside

Look inside you

THE DESCENT

2005-2015

2005

From: Tina Greer
Date: September 26, 2005 1:18 PM
To: Mary Greer
Subject: FW

By the way, I knew you had to get to the video store yesterday, but I wanted to ask you how Michelle was doing. Last I heard was you thought she was having a breakdown before you went to Florida.

2007

From: Mary Greer
Date: December 19, 2007 10:52 AM
To: Marc Charles
Subject: FW: Friday the 21st MORE

Just talked to Malcolm—he can't do Sunday so will see me and the kids and dad on Friday night. What time on Sunday—do you just want to come here and hang out? And do you mind if I ask Michelle to come? I think she would like to see you.

From: Marc Charles
Date: December 19, 2007 10:55 AM
To: Mary Greer
Subject: RE: Friday the 21st MORE

How about Sunday afternoon around 2 pm? Just a get together to say hello and give the kids some gifts? If Michelle is sober, that's fine; if she isn't, I think we need to team up and tell her to leave. I'll drive her home if need be.

From: Mary Greer
Date: December 19, 2007 11:43 AM
To: Marc Charles
Subject: RE: Friday the 21st MORE

Sunday at 2 is fine. I don't think I will ask Michelle at all—asking her to leave is really not an option in front of the kids.

From: Marc Charles
Date: December 19, 2007 11:50 AM
To: Mary Greer
Subject: RE: Friday the 21st MORE

Ok, 2 pm is good - I'll be there. As I mentioned earlier, Christine's staying close by her mother this weekend because of her father, so it will just be me this year. As far as Michelle is concerned, I haven't seen her all year, but Dad tells me she has obvious issues these days. I'd be glad to see her, but I don't want to pretend everything is fine if she's obviously not sober while I'm there. If you think it's too risky to invite her, then I'm fine with that. I hope that makes some sense.

From: Marc Charles
Date: December 20, 2007 12:03 PM
To: Mary Greer
Subject: RE: Friday the 21st MORE

My suggestion would be to give her a chance by inviting her . . . If she's not in good shape, I will quietly let her know she isn't fooling anyone and suggest she do the right thing by going home. There doesn't need to be a scene.

From: Mary Greer
Date: December 20, 2007 12:40 PM
To: Marc Charles
Subject: RE: Friday the 21st MORE

Let me mull on this for a bit. I really don't think if you say something to her there is any way she is going to just leave quietly.

From: Marc Charles
Date: December 20, 2007 12:55 PM
To: Mary Greer
Subject: Friday the 21st MORE

I doubt there would be a scene. I've mentioned it to her to her face before, and she's quietly said "she had a bad night" the night before . . . Have you seen her lately? I haven't, in months. Do you suspect there's a good chance she'll show up under the influence?

2008

From: Marc Charles
Date: May 5, 2008 9:59 AM
To: Mary Greer; Malcolm Charles
Subject: Michelle

Here's a place that could provide us with a trained intervention counselor:
http://www.serenity.org/intervenestrategies.htm
They are having an intervention specialist call me back this afternoon. I will let you know how it goes.

From: Mary Greer
Date: May 5, 2008 10:08 AM
To: Marc Charles; Malcolm Charles
Subject: RE: Michelle

She is seeing her doctor at 11:30 this morning. Would not let me go–*completely* overwrought/nearly hysterical. She is going to call me after it is over and tell me what the doctor recommends. If we don't think it is adequate, I think we move forward with an intervention.

From: Marc Charles
Date: May 5, 2008 10:17 AM
To: Mary Greer; Malcolm Charles
Subject: RE: Michelle

Her psychiatrist you mean? That guy (Wilford?) in the city she used to see?

From: Mary Greer
Date: May 5, 2008 10:17 AM
To: Marc Charles
Cc: Malcolm Charles
Subject: RE: Michelle

No, he died about five years ago. She is seeing her primary care doctor; she is going to need referrals for whatever is decided (outpatient, hospitalization, whatever). She is also going to ask to be referred to another psychiatrist.

From: Marc Charles
Date: May 5, 2008 10:30 AM
To: Mary Greer
Cc: Malcolm Charles
Subject: RE: Michelle

Good . . .

The intervention counselor called me back; she seemed well-informed and competent. The intervention would involve two "prep" meetings of two hours each (without Michelle), and then the intervention meeting itself with Michelle (maybe another couple of hours).

She had some interesting insight, such as using a more "objective" relative (such as Liam) as the intervention chairperson, and having everyone read pre-written letters to Michelle at the meeting (rather than ad-libbing it).

The cost would be $200 per hour; and we would expect to need about six hours to conduct the whole process (or $1200).

This is not a prohibitive cost from my perspective; Malcolm, let me know what you think. Mary, I know you are buried in the kids' school costs so don't worry about it for now.

The woman is sending more details to me via e-mail today, which I will forward to you both. I suggest we have Plan B primed and ready to go if Michelle's own efforts look like they are misguided.

From: Marc Charles
Date: May 5, 2008 10:33 AM
To: Mary Greer
Cc: Malcolm Charles
Subject: RE: Michelle

One other note on the intervention process... The counselor also said the two prep meetings and the intervention itself could be conducted over a long weekend, for example starting with a Friday night prep meeting and finishing up with the intervention meeting itself on Sunday or Monday. Malcolm: that might enable you to participate without missing too much work time.

From: Malcolm Charles
Date: May 5, 2008 10:38 AM
To: Marc Charles; Mary Greer
Subject: RE: Michelle

That cost is fine with me - a long weekend would be great. If the prep can't be over a long weekend, I can come up for at least one of the prep meetings and of course the intervention itself; and I think Liam chairing is a good idea. What is important, I think, is to ask what we do if/when Michelle shows up, realizes what we're doing, and simply leaves/refuses to participate. Also, if by some miracle she stays in the same room w/us, we need to make sure Richard doesn't flake out and buy into her behavior or otherwise undermine the intervention.

Also, do we do this if Michelle is admitted this afternoon/this week? I would think so, but in any case, I think it's important we consider the most likely scenarios starting now.

From: Marc Charles
Date: May 5, 2008 10:45 AM
To: Malcolm Charles; Mary Greer
Subject: RE: Michelle

I'd be surprised if a doctor authorized admission to any serious treatment facility this week. If so, that's great, and we would let that treatment run its course. We would let the counselor decide if Dad should or should not be part of the intervention. If she felt he would be a liability, we would leave him at home.

From: Marc Charles
Date: May 5, 2008, 10:52 AM
To: Mary Greer; Malcolm Charles
Subject: Michelle

Here's the intervention information from Serenity. It is not an easy process.

From: Marc Charles
Date: May 7, 2008 9:09 AM
To: Mary Greer; Malcolm Charles
Subject: Michelle

Do we know the name of the doctor she is dealing with? I'd like to call him as "next of kin" and find out what the plan is.

From: Marc Charles
Date: May 7, 2008 11:02 AM
To: Mary Greer
Cc: Malcolm Charles
Subject: RE: Michelle

More good news - Her doctor has lost a malpractice award and has also been suspended in the past.

From: Marc Charles
To: Richard Charles; Mary Greer; Malcolm Charles
Date: May 8, 2008 5:11 PM
Subject: Suggestion

Dad / Mary / Malcolm - I think the four of us (me, Malcolm, Dad, Mary) should go ahead with a couple of meetings with the counselor from Serenity next week (hopefully Friday and Saturday). Michelle will hopefully be in a hospital by then, but I think the four of us still need professional advice on how to handle this mess. For example, should she be helped with food shopping, the car repairs, getting to meetings, etc., or should she be left alone to sort it all out herself? Frankly, we don't know the right answers, and I think we need a professional to tell us how to proceed for the next 30 days.

Malcolm has agreed to participate (again, hopefully the Friday a week from tomorrow), and he and I will handle the costs. Does this make sense to you? If we can get the counselor booked for the weekend of May 17, can you all participate?

From: Malcolm Charles
Date: May 8, 2008 5:18 PM
To: Marc Charles; Richard Charles; Mary Greer
Subject: Re: Suggestion

Thanks, Marc, for taking the lead on this.

Good questions, Marc. One common-sense thing: We should NOT help with car repairs - if anyone is helping her with that, STOP. We need a professional to guide us through this but I'm shocked that anyone would help her get her car fixed in all this mess.

I'll be there for the meeting or meetings - this is extremely serious.

Malcolm

From: Mary Greer
Date: May 20, 2008 8:26 AM
To: Tina Greer
Subject: RE: Dad

Also, we miraculously managed to get Michelle into a hospital on Thursday. She lasted two days and said she was leaving. To create a united front, we all said we would not pick her up (figuring that would force her to stay), so she took a bus!!! Marc and my father went to see one of their counselors and they basically said to leave her alone and don't help her unless she agrees to go to treatment. But otherwise, she said there is not much you can do. It has to come from her. We probably have enough to have a judge force her into the hospital, but they don't recommend that because it hasn't come from the person and tends to create more problems instead of solving them. In some ways, it is good to have someone tell us that and now we are all on the same page. However, it feels very uncomfortable knowing she is out there and not knowing what she is going to get up to next.

Anyway, if you hear any more about your father let us know. I hope he can get out to see you soon—he really needs these trips and the contact. Love, Mary

2009

From: Mary Greer
Date: June 1, 2009 9:02 AM
To: Tina Greer
Subject: Any news?

Tina,
My sister was just committed for 30 days to Hightower. It is a very bad situation—her probation officer (yes, she has a probation officer; apparently, she had a second DUI we didn't know about) said she doesn't think just de-tox is going to work. She thinks Michelle has a very significant mental illness. Not sure what is going to happen.

Love, Mary

From: Mary Greer
To: Marc Charles
Date: November 2, 2009 11:58 AM
Subject: Times

Hi, Marc,
As you requested, below are times I am available to go down to Social Security with Michelle.

This week
Between 9 and 2 (need to be done by 2 each day to go pick up Jamie) on Thursday or Friday

Next week (w/o 11/9-11/13)
Between 9 and 2 on Monday, Tuesday, Thursday, or Friday (Wed is Veteran's Day)

The week after that (w/o 11/16-11/18)
Between 9 and 2 on Monday or Tuesday. Might be able to do Thursday or Friday, Jamie will have a pre-assigned teacher conference on one of those days, I just don't have the time or day yet–will let you know.

From: Marc Charles
To: Mary Greer
Date: November 6, 2009 12:02 PM
Subject: Re: Times

Mary - Michelle set up an appt. with a soc. sec. office for Thurs, Dec. 3 at 9 am. If you can go, great, if not, it's not the end of the world.

From: Mary Greer
To: Marc Charles
Date: November 6, 2009 1:51 PM
Subject: Re: Times

Unless something unforeseen happens, I can do this. I will just meet her there at that time.

From: Marc Charles
To: Mary Greer
Date: November 6, 2009 2:00 PM
Subject: Re: Times

Ok, great . . .

From: Mary Greer
To: Marc Charles
Date: November 6, 2009 3:30 PM
Subject: Re: Times

Marc,
I just went thru the packet you sent. Quick question, the Transitional Assistance section–I am not doing that right now, right? We are kicking everything off at the appt on Dec 3 instead?

Mary

From: Marc Charles
To: Mary Greer
Date: November 6, 2009 3:36 PM
Subject: Re: Times

Yes, the DTA stuff is just for the state program, and Michelle is so far handling that application herself. I included it to show you the type of language we used to try to make her case for assistance (I wrote all of the comments you see in it).

For the SSI appointment, I would bring the Hightower records and a copy of the DTA application to use as a reference, just in case you or Michelle are struggling to explain her disability to the SSI representative.

From: Marc Charles
To: Mary Greer
Date: December 1, 2009 5:48 PM
Subject: Re: Xmas

Mary - Are you all set for the SSI appointment with Michelle?

You really have four objectives:

1) Take notes and fully understand what the SSI person is telling Michelle. Keep a list of any additional information they will need to collect from her. Michelle sometimes misses important details in conversations like this.

2) Keep Michelle focused on the questions she's being asked. She sometimes fails to answer a question, and instead digresses into the many problems or injustices she faces. The rep will need clear/specific answers to the specific questions he/she asks.

3) Have the Hightower medical documents ready in case Michelle struggles with an answer. Offer to share them with the SSI rep. The records explain her issues far better than Michelle can.

4) Review the follow-up notes and "to-do" list with Michelle right after the meeting, to make sure she knows what additional documents she'll need to collect. They may also send her to a doctor for an evaluation.

Let's talk on the phone tomorrow or Thursday to review... Thanks for helping out with this.

From: Mary Greer
To: Marc Charles
Date: December 1, 2009 7:00 PM
Subject: Re: Xmas

Marc,
I'm glad you emailed–yes, let's talk tomorrow. Got it on the objectives–will bring the packet you sent. Questions: Should I call her to just confirm? I feel strange just meeting her there, but maybe that way is best? Also, is this at the regular SS office?
PS: Just got your card. Thanks. 50–yikes!

From: Marc Charles
To: Mary Greer
Date: December 1, 2009 9:14 PM
Subject: Re: Xmas

Yes, feel free to call me. I will confirm the appt. with her, the address, and that you will be there, but you can call her beforehand if you'd like. She's been aware for several weeks that you'll be involved in this.

From: Marc Charles
To: Mary Greer
Date: December 14, 2009 2:33 PM
Subject: Dec-14

Hi Mary - I have a message in to Michelle about the lunch invitation, and also about following up with the court on the Mendoza default issue. I will keep you posted. What would be good gifts for Jamie and Joni this year? I'm running out of time, as usual!

Nothing for me and Christine this year please; I'm going to be pretty stingy myself this year about getting other people gifts. The issues with Michelle really hit hard.

From: Mary Greer
To: Marc Charles
Date: December 15, 2009 8:46 AM
Subject: Re: Dec-14

Marc,
I know they would love a zip line. I have attached a link to one on Amazon that is in stock, and if you choose overnight shipping, you could have it by tomorrow. I know you would get the happy "Christmas dance." They have wanted one for years and we just never got around to it.

Also, it is now pretty clear Michelle is not going to be here on Saturday. Are you (and/or) Christine going to come by? Here is the schedule:

7am open gifts/Santa is here
10am Bob Cannon and Dad here-brunch
play with new toys for the afternoon
4pm Chinese food
7pm watch Polar Express/popcorn and cocoa

From: Marc Charles
To: Mary Greer
Date: December 15, 2009 5:50 PM
Subject: Re: Dec-14

No word from Michelle yet. I will have Dad drive by if I don't hear something soon. I ordered the gift! Christine and I are planning on getting there between 2 and 3 pm. What would be a good small gift for Bob Cannon?

From: Mary Greer
To: Marc Charles
Date: December 16, 2009 8:47 AM
Subject: Re: Dec-14

Yes, I am getting concerned if she did not respond to you, either. Have you sent her money or anything that she has cashed/processed (i.e., some way of knowing that she is ok)?

Regarding Bob, don't get him anything. He has a dinner to go to someplace else that night, so I am pretty sure he will be gone by the time you arrive. If not, he won't have anything for you either, so it would just embarrass him if you brought him something.

From: Marc Charles
To: Mary Greer
Date: December 16, 2009 6:09 PM
Subject: Re: Dec-14

Dad just knocked on Michelle's door to check in (I asked him to). She's fine, she had the damn cell phone shut off because some bill collector kept calling.

2010

From: Marc Charles
To: Mary Greer
Date: January 14, 2010 5:16 PM
Subject: Re: Fwd: From today's Times

Thanks - I've read other stories on-line that say he's been fined many times by various regulators (town & state), and never pays, and no one ever prosecutes or punishes him. Michelle walked into a terrible situation when she bought that place because her judgment was impaired by her various issues, and because she didn't ask anyone for help/advice before she bought it. It's a nightmare, but she really set herself up for it.

From: Mary Greer
Date: February 4, 2010 7:21 AM
To: Tina Greer
Subject: Re: update

Tina,
Michelle is doing better (not great, but certainly better). Baby steps . . . . We are going to church with her Saturday, which is HUGE. Still no progress on employment, though she is volunteering at the library, which is definitely a move in the right direction. Anyway, let me know if you can talk today.

Love, Mary

From: Mary Greer
Date: February 10, 2010 1:59 PM
To: Tina Greer
Subject: Update

Hey, Tina,

Speaking of which, I didn't tell you when we spoke but church with my sister was a disaster. She showed up smelling strongly of alcohol. I was very upset—not just that she is drinking but that she was driving. She has two DUIs already; one more and she goes to jail. Marc is paying for her car on the condition that she get a job (which she has not done). He is probably going to let her car get repo'ed. Not to be mean, but because she is a danger to herself and to others. We don't even know where she is getting the money to buy booze since she has no income (Marc pays her bills directly). My father sends her gas cards and cartons of cigarettes and we think maybe she is selling them. Who knows, but Marc told him to stop for now. Very upsetting to say the least. Hopefully this is one of those slip-ups on the way to recovery. I really felt like she was making progress.

From: Marc Charles
To: Mary Greer, Richard Charles
Date: February 19, 2010 12:45 PM
Subject: Call

Can we try to do a brief conference call on Monday to talk about next steps with Michelle? There is no big news to report, but we should probably start planning for some changes. I'm only tied up on Monday from 11 to 12 and from 4 to 5.

From: Mary Greer
To: Marc Charles
Cc: Richard Charles
Date: February 19, 2010 12:53 PM
Subject: Re: Call

I am having surgery on Monday. I have to be there at 6:30am and won't be home until Tuesday at the earliest. Can you do it Sunday or do you need to be in your office for the conference call capability? If not Sunday, I probably won't be able to think very clearly until Thursday due to the pain medications. Could it wait until then? I would be free any time that day.

From: Marc Charles
To: Mary Greer
Cc: Richard Charles
Date: February 19, 2010 1:07 PM
Subject: Re: Call

I forgot about the surgery. Let's wait a week until you're feeling better. Things haven't really changed with Michelle; I just want to start planning ahead. Maybe we could even wait until next Friday. I tend to have more time available on Fridays.

From: Mary Greer
To: Marc Charles
Cc: Richard Charles
Date: February 19, 2010 1:11 PM
Subject: Re: Call

Friday would be fine. I will just be lying around so anytime is fine. Have you seen or talked to Michelle recently?

From: Marc Charles
To: Mary Greer
Cc: Richard Charles
Date: February 19, 2010 3:25 PM
Subject: Re: Call

I talked to her last night. No big news, but nothing has really changed: no job, no prospects, etc.

From: Marc Charles
To: Richard Charles, Mary Greer
Date: March 30, 2010 9:26 AM
Subject: March_30

Dad - Are there any days that you will not be working this week or early next week? I'd like to have a call about Michelle.

From: Mary Greer
To: Marc Charles
Date: March 30, 2010 12:03 PM
Subject: Re: March_30

Hey, Marc,
Did something else happen, or is this about the car? I am available any day next week, so long as it is between 9am-2pm.

From: Marc Charles
To: Richard Charles
Date: April 13, 2010 1:56 PM
Subject: Appointment

Dad / Mary - Can either of you go with Michelle to see her state health counselor (I think she's an LSW) on Friday, April 23rd? I will get the exact time & place from Michelle tomorrow. I will prepare a "script" or talking points for whomever winds up going with her. As we have discussed, the objective is to stress to her health care professionals the urgency of Michelle getting in to see a qualified psychiatrist on a regular basis (which hasn't happened yet, despite the fact that she has been enrolled for about nine months). I'll also mail to each of you the key one-page summary that Hightower wrote up when she was discharged last June, and highlight the key statements that would be of interest to the people you will be talking to.

From: Richard Charles
To: Marc Charles
Cc: Mary Greer
Date: April 13, 2010 2:06 PM
Subject: Re: Appointment

I would be glad to go, of course; but I think Mary could do a better job simply because she is more educated and can discuss matters much more intelligently than me. But will be glad to go if Mary can't or doesn't want to. Dad

From: Marc Charles
To: Richard Charles
Cc: Mary Greer
Date: April 13, 2010 2:10 PM
Subject: Re: Appointment

You should both keep in mind that you only need to attend the first 5 minutes of the appointment, to stress the urgency of the situation and to plead for a psychiatrist's appointment. Then you can leave. You don't need to sit through the entire counseling session.

From: Richard Charles
To: Marc Charles
Cc: Mary Greer
Date: April 13, 2010 2:16 PM
Subject: Re: Appointment

OK - If you both think I can handle it, I would be glad to go.

From: Marc Charles
To: Richard Charles
Date: April 13, 2010 5:39 PM
Subject: May 10

Just looking ahead, the next hearing for the divorce/alimony issue is on Monday, May 10. I went to the last one, so it would be great if one of you could attend this one. It basically involves taking good notes on everything the judge and attorneys say. Michelle has a tendency to forget or misinterpret some important information at these things.

From: Richard Charles
To: Marc Charles, Mary Greer
Date: April 13, 2010 6:10 PM
Subject: Re: May 10

OK - I'll go – Dad

From: <LAWYER>
To: Marc Charles
Date: April 18, 2010 2:16 PM
Subject: Michelle Jackson

Attached please find a letter received from <LAWYER> dated April 7, 2010 for your review and comments.

Thank you,
Paralegal

From: Marc Charles
To: Richard Charles, Mary Greer, Malcolm Charles
Date: August 18, 2010 2:39 PM
Subject: FW: Michelle Jackson

For discussion. I'm interested in your opinions on what is being offered.

From: Malcolm Charles
To: Marc Charles
Cc: Richard Charles, Mary Greer
Date: August 18, 2010 3:01 PM
Subject: Re: FW: Michelle Jackson

Marc, thanks for sending along. I don't know the legal merits of either Michelle's or Nicholas's positions, but it sounds like the 50k will allow Nicholas to wash his hands of any future payments to Michelle, whether for alimony, insurance, etc. In other words, if she accepts this 50k she'd have no legal leg to stand on if she tries to sue later on to get something else from him? Is that correct?

That said, unless it's earmarked for something else (debts, rent, etc.), which is being handled by you, Marc, I assume Michelle will burn through this cash in no time flat and be in exactly the same position within a matter of months, with nothing in her life resolved or fixed. Unless I'm not up to date on any new developments with her. My key question is if this will contribute to her recovery or if this will allow her to continue to ruin her life - I assumed when I saw your email with her name in the subject that this was something police related or an email notification of her death.

Malcolm

From: Marc Charles
To: Mary Greer
Date: September 27, 2010 5:02 PM
Subject: Sept-27

Mary - Just a heads up - Michelle mentioned to me the other day that there was some sort of class she was interested in taking. You should be aware that I flatly told her no, that she couldn't afford to spend one cent on any classes or schooling.

Unlike most people, Michelle has a long track record of not using her schooling to get ahead in the workforce (or to work at all for that matter). She already has a B.A., but she's made no effort to use it at all over the last 12-15 years. She also obtained a paralegal certificate a few years ago, but once again did absolutely nothing useful with it.

She is still sitting in a very, very desperate financial situation, and it will likely stay that way for the rest of her life, even if she gets a small settlement from Nicholas (which is still not close to being a certainty).

For the foreseeable future, therefore, she simply needs to work, and work very hard. I would love to think that some classes would make her situation better, or that she will finally "apply herself" if she obtains another certificate of some sort, but I am absolutely convinced it will not play out that way. Her track record of counter-productive behavior, even after some pretty decent education, is blatant.

I wish I had an easier answer for her, but I don't. I just wanted to make sure you were aware.

From: Mary Greer
To: Marc Charles
Date: September 29, 2010 1:53 PM
Subject: Re: Sept-27

I totally understand–was trying to help/inspire (she is very depressed and it is hard to listen without offering suggestions that might make the future seem like it might get better) but you are right.

Am also not at all sure if she is really not drinking, but at least she has held the job for a while–it would be great if she could get it to full time. I wonder sometimes, despite her protestations, if she just does not want full time, or if it really is not available.

I will keep quiet except to reiterate that mantra. She needs to focus on work. Period.

From: Mary Greer
To: Marc Charles
Date: October 21, 2010 10:24 AM
Subject: Re: M.C.

Hey, Marc–responses below each para.
----- Original Message -----

From: Marc Charles
To: Mary Greer
Date: October 20, 2010 9:59 AM
Subject: M.C.

Hi Mary - Got your voicemail yesterday. We'd be glad to meet you guys for dinner Saturday night or afternoon. There's a big shopping area we could go to - It has a Friday's, Uno's, Applebee's, Red Robin, Longhorn Steakhouse, Cold Stone Creamery, etc. Just let us know.

Ok, great. My guys love Red Robin, so how about Red Robin at 5? Also, what is the name of the plaza?

On the caroling event, are you doing that in lieu of a Christmas gathering later in the month (because of your Florida trip)? I forgot what you told me . . .

No, we are still doing a family Christmas the weekend (probably on Saturday) before we leave on the 22nd (so the kids can have their presents, stockings, Santa, etc.). Dad will come, and likely Michelle too. I can see that you might not want to come down twice—if you wanted to just come to the caroling, maybe I could see if Dad wanted to go to that, and you could give him his gift then? Or forget the caroling and just come for the Christmas thing the weekend before. The only reason I mentioned the caroling is that we were so impressed last year—it is really quite special. I can't believe we haven't been doing it all along.

One other thing - Christine asked if you have a copy (or negative) of the big "four siblings" photograph that Liam took of all of us about 20 years ago (the one that hung on the wall at Dad's house for years). She likes it for some reason!

The picture I have was actually Mom's. I had two made at the time-one for her and one for Dad because they were already divorced. I think Dad still has his, but maybe he would let you have it? As for the actual photo, I think Michelle ended up taking all the original photos that were taken; not sure if the one we blew up is part of that group. Do you want me to ask her? I could also ask Dad if you want me to see if he would let you have his.

Hope all is well . . . Take care.

From: Marc Charles
To: Mary Greer
Date: October 21, 2010 11:23 AM
Subject: Re: M.C.

The Red Robin is at The Shoppes. It's a big outdoor mall. 5 pm should be good; I'll double-check with Christine.

Maybe we'll do the caroling event with you instead of coming down on the 18th. I think it's a good idea to bring Michelle to these events now, but I myself need a break from her this year. By the way, an IRA transfer has now been signed by Nicholas for $91K. She gets taxed heavily if she withdraws from the new account, but at least it's something.

Don't worry about the photo. I don't want to take Dad's from him. Eventually I'll ask Michelle to dig through her stuff to see if she still has the smaller version of it.

2011

From: Marc Charles
To: Mary Greer
Date: February 23, 2011 9:52 AM
Subject: Transfer

Mary - Dad's transfer is all set for tomorrow morning. Will you and/or Liam be able to shuttle him across town any time before noon? I presume The Manor will let you borrow the folding wheelchair again. The only other thing they will need from you is his health care cards (Medicare, Blue Cross Medex Bronze, Blue Cross drug plan Part D, and Delta Dental). I'll fax over the Health Care Proxy form tomorrow morning, and I'll notify the hospital doctors that he's moving. Let me know if this works for you.

From: Mary Greer
To: Marc Charles
Date: February 23, 2011 10:04 AM
Subject: Re: Transfer

I could do it between 1 and 4–will that work? If not, can Michelle do it? I have two kids home on school vacation and I am also working. We are in for a long slog here and I cannot keep it up–she is going to have to do more.

From: Marc Charles
To: Mary Greer
Date: February 23, 2011 10:08 AM
Subject: Re: Transfer

Any time between 1 and 4 is fine. Michelle unfortunately is the wrong person for this (if you'd like, I can give you a couple of very, very recent examples of how irresponsible and immature she really is). If worse comes to worst, we can always have The Manor arrange transport (probably for a small charge, $150 or so, not the end of the world) . . . . Just let me know, so I can let them know the plan.

From: Mary Greer
To: Marc Charles
Date: February 25, 2011 10:41 AM
Subject: Resched Appt

Good news–they rescheduled for this Monday, Feb 28 at 10am. I will take him.

From: Marc Charles
To: Mary Greer, Malcolm Charles
Date: April 6, 2011 12:30 PM
Subject: National Cemetery

The guy from the funeral home just called. He said Dad's ashes have been delivered to him already. He now wants us to give him a date and time to hold the ceremony at National Cemetery. A military soldier will be present, so he needs us to be specific. I know Mary's away the weekend of the 16th, so let's come up with some alternatives. Malcolm, it's up to you whether you want to drive up here again or not for this.

From: Mary Greer
To: Marc Charles
Cc: Malcolm Charles
Date: April 6, 2011 12:38 PM
Subject: Re: National Cemetery

We are flexible—let me see what Malcolm wants/can do. I will then call Michelle as I know she wants to be there. Do you want me to pick up the ashes ahead of time so we have them for the canal?

From: Mary Greer
To: Marc Charles
Date: April 6, 2011 4:11 PM
Subject: Michelle's Letter

. . . did not arrive.

From: Marc Charles
To: Mary Greer, Malcolm Charles
Date: April 8, 2011 11:58 AM
Subject: Computer

Is anyone going to want Dad's computer or printer? If not, the PC's hard drive is going to have to be erased or destroyed. It likely contains his social security number, tax and bank records, etc. Please let me know if you want it. Otherwise I'll make preparations to destroy.

From: Mary Greer
To: Marc Charles, Malcolm Charles
Date: April 8, 2011 2:46 PM
Subject: Re: Computer

Michelle might want it—shall I ask her? By the way, she did pick up that letter this morning.

From: Mary Greer
To: Marc Charles
Date: April 22, 2011 1:59 PM
Subject: Michelle

I just got a voice mail from her asking for gas money. Thoughts?

From: Marc Charles
To: Mary Greer, Malcolm Charles
Date: June 7, 2011 11:48 AM
Subject: Friday

I just talked to the funeral home - We should meet there at 8:30 on Friday. We will then go with them to the cemetery for the service at 9 AM. I reminded them about the two urns. They also told me to remember to bring the flag they gave us at the calling hours (which I still have). We will not be seeing the actual burial or placing of the stone. The military honors are instead done near a small chapel at the entrance to the cemetery. A few weeks later, the marker will be placed and we'll be able to go and see it whenever we like. Please feel free to give me a call if need be.

From: Mary Greer
To: Marc Charles
Date: June 7, 2011 11:55 AM
Subject: Re: Friday

Ok, have you talked to Malcolm? Is he coming? And are we just going to go to the canal right after? And finally, would you want to go out for lunch before you head back?

From: Marc Charles
To: Mary Greer
Date: June 11, 2011 5:09 PM
Subject: Re: Friday

No idea about Malcolm - He's certainly been reminded of the date more than once over the last few weeks. Yes, let's go to the canal after the service, and then we can have lunch somewhere. Feel free to remind Michelle, but I can tell you that she was having some sort of meltdown as of a week ago. Her landlord called me at work and said she had strewn garbage all over the yard in back of her unit. Apparently it was a childish temper tantrum, most likely under the influence.

If she acts up on Friday, or smells of alcohol, I will tell her to leave.

From: Marc Charles
To: Mary Greer
Date: July 14, 2011 4:26 PM
Subject: July-14

Hear from Michelle lately? I talked to her yesterday to ask if the trailer needed a power wash, and got a familiar routine of paranoid ramblings about her landlord, the repeating of the same phrases over and over, etc., etc. She did not sound well, but is apparently still employed. If you've talked to her, let me know.

I frankly am having a hard time picturing her living productively and safely in anything other than some sort of monitored living situation over the long-term. She appears to be incapable of functioning as an adult on her own. She makes decisions and reacts to difficult situations with no more maturity (or intelligence) than a 12-year-old child. That is not an exaggeration. On top of it all, she has a well-documented drinking problem that stills seems to be a serious issue.

I don't know what the answer will or should be, but I am not optimistic at this point. Even when she is not under the influence of alcohol, she sounds like she is mentally ill (rambling about the landlords out to get her, the local/town political conspiracies, etc.). You get the distinct feeling that you are talking to a certifiable crazy person when you speak with her. It's very troubling.

Don't mean to ruin your day, but honesty is probably a good idea at this point. Her future is not bright. I'm open to any and all ideas at this point, because I don't know what's going to happen to her. Feel free to share this with Malcolm as well. He ought to at least be aware that his sister is not functioning and is at risk.

From: Mary Greer
To: Marc Charles
Date: July 14, 2011 4:53 PM
Subject: Re: July-14

Let's talk by phone. I have talked to her and she sounded ok (not great, but ok). But I always talk to her when she is at work because she calls me on her break, so she is definitely sober. When she repeats phrases over and over it ALWAYS means she is drunk. I have always found it troubling that she was not in AA. All the documents I edit for my consulting work all say the same thing–substance abuse will persist without treatment, and the only treatment that works is groups (i.e., AA). My opinion is that you should tell her you will not pay her rent unless she goes to AA. She cannot stop drinking on her own, and that is going to land her in jail. I agree she has mental problems, but it is impossible to drill down to what they are because of the substance abuse.

From: Marc Charles
To: Mary Greer
Date: July 22, 2011 11:35 PM
Subject: Location

Mary - Dad's marker is in Section 54, and its marker #86. I'm sure the people at the front gate can point you in the right direction if you visit there.

From: Mary Greer
To: Marc Charles
Date: July 26, 2011 7:46 AM
Subject: Location

Thanks, Also, I think I should have Liam go over Michelle's and resolve the power wash situation. She called again about it and I think it is really beyond her ability to cope (to get estimates and handle it in any way). Ok with you for me to call her and get this arranged? I just want to get it dealt with and frankly, I feel bad about it.

Mary

From: Marc Charles
To: Mary Greer
Date: July 26, 2011 9:20 AM
Subject: Re: Location

I'm fine with Liam LOOKING at the exterior and deciding whether or not it needs a power wash. I will pay someone else to do the work, however. Let's save Liam's time and energy for something more important, which I'm sure will come up soon enough.

It is also worthwhile to use situations like this to reinforce to Michelle that there is no "free lunch." Taking care of a home and supporting yourself costs money; hence, one needs to work for a living. She needs to learn that.

From: Marc Charles
To: Mary Greer
Date: August 5, 2011 9:17 AM
Subject: Aug-13th

Mary - I'm considering driving down on Saturday the 13th to look at the exterior of Michelle's house and sweep some branches and pine needles off of her roof. She says the roof needs a cleaning much more than the walls need a power washing. Would Liam be willing to meet me there with a ladder and a broom at around 6 pm? I suspect it will only take about an hour to get all the crap off the roof. I'm not going to hang around there, and I suspect Michelle will be working. I'll obviously let her know what we're up to beforehand. She attempted to line up a contractor to do the power washing this week, but I looked the guy up on the internet and made her cancel it. He looked very shady (brushes with the law, etc.). So the power washing is on hold for a while. The roof sweeping sounds like an easy project though, and I want to take a look at it myself. Let me know what Liam thinks. Very sorry to inconvenience him with this stuff.

From: Mary Greer
To: Marc Charles
Cc: Liam Greer
Date: August 5, 2011 9:47 AM
Subject: Re: Aug-13th

Yes, that will be fine; it is on the calendar. Am cc'ing Liam so he will remember the ladder and broom. Also, he said he will bring his power washer, just in case it is worth taking care of on the spot. Do you have a key to the trailer, in case you need a water source?

From: Marc Charles
To: Mary Greer
Date: August 5, 2011 5:50 PM
Subject: Re: Aug-13th

Ok, thanks. I have a message in to Michelle to leave her outside water on that day (like a hose). I'll talk to her before then either way.

From: Marc Charles
To: Mary Greer
Date: August 7, 2011 2:28 PM
Subject: Re: Aug-13th

Mary - How does Liam feel about 5:30 pm instead of 6 on Saturday night? I want to try to get back on the road by 7 pm.

From: Mary Greer
To: Marc Charles
Date: August 7, 2011 2:48 PM
Subject: Re: Aug-13th

It would be better–the earlier the better. If it can be even earlier than 5:30 let me know.

From: Marc Charles
To: Mary Greer
Date: August 11, 2011 5:58 PM
Subject: Re: Aug-13th

Hi Mary - Liam still all set for 5:30 pm on Saturday? I'm looking forward to it . . . Bringing my own broom for the roof actually.

From: Mary Greer
To: Marc Charles
Date: August 11, 2011 6:44 PM
Subject: Re: Aug-13th

Yes.

On another topic, I was also going to email you because I talked to Malcolm today after weeks of him not returning my calls. You had asked me to tell him how badly Michelle was doing, which I did. He is now very angry at me for saying I don't want to go to AA with Michelle because the island is such a small community and I don't want people to see me there, assume I am the alcoholic, and have it affect my kids. What do you think? Should I ask her if she would go if I went with her? Maybe we could go off-island–I don't know . . . .

Mary

From: Marc Charles
To: Mary Greer
Date: August 12, 2011 11:20 AM
Subject: Re: Aug-13th

As far as AA is concerned, while it would be wonderful if you or I (or both) accompanied her to meetings, I confess that the logistics are almost out of the question for me, and I completely understand your own reasons for not wanting to attend. I don't think either one of us is obligated to feel guilty about this. Michelle needs to attend, and needs to WANT to attend.

I think the next best thing that either one of us can do is confront her on the issue each time we "catch" her when she's under the influence (or a day later, when she's lucid). She's unfortunately very cagey about this, and hard to catch in the act, but she should be called on it every time there's a reasonable suspicion.

I wish I had better answers, but I don't. That's why I called you a few weeks ago; the problem seems to be unsolvable (at least by you and me). This week, as I've reminded Michelle that Liam and I were coming by, she's been absolutely fine, lucid, alert, etc. That makes it all the more difficult to know how to deal with her drinking problem. You just never know when it's going to pop up again.

Let's talk on the phone if you want. This is unfortunately a frustrating problem that never seems to get fixed, no matter how much time, money, and effort you put into it.

From: Marc Charles
To: Mary Greer
Date: August 15, 2011 7:57 PM
Subject: Thanks

Mary - Please thank Liam for me for doing such a fantastic job on Michelle's trailer. It desperately needed the power wash. Liam blasted through the whole thing in about an hour and a half. Please tell him I appreciate it. As for Michelle, she sounded ok on the phone this weekend, but boy is she clueless. She didn't think her trailer needed the cleaning, yet it was a complete mess. I think she's too lazy to confront any sort of problem (or chore) whatsoever. Anyway, I owe Liam a dinner or something. Please no word to Christine on this. She doesn't want to hear about me doing Michelle any favors.

From: Marc Charles
To: Mary Greer
Date: September 13, 2011 10:28 PM
Subject: Message

Mary - Got your voicemail today - I haven't heard from Michelle in several days either. Let's give it another day and we can both try calling her again. Past experience suggests she is just in a bad mood, or has had a relapse with the alcohol, but reaching out to her is still a good idea. Please check in with me tomorrow afternoon.

From: Mary Greer
To: Marc Charles
Date: September 14, 2011 8:35 AM
Subject: Re: Message

I talked to her yesterday. She's ok–not great but status quo. Hates her job, hates where she lives, etc. There was some repetitiveness to her speech and she wasn't working, so I do suspect she was drinking. But I'm not sure. And I did not say anything about that over-55 trailer park. Just wanted you to see it so we could start exploring options. Four years is a long time to wait though.

From: Marc Charles
To: Mary Greer
Date: September 14, 2011 3:36 PM
Subject: Re: Message

She really hates her job, or does she hate the fact that they will only give her 20 hours per week?

From: Mary Greer
To: Marc Charles
Date: September 14, 2011 4:28 PM
Subject: Re: Message

I think she hates the actual job–I am getting a little concerned that she may be giving them a bit of attitude now that she is getting more comfortable. She told me that she asked them not to put her on the register–to let her work in the aisles (stocking shelves, etc.). She started out as totally enthusiastic to them in the hopes that they would think she was awesome and they would put her on full time; I don't think that is the face she is putting forth now. But, the fact is, I really don't know.

From: Marc Charles
To: Mary Greer
Date: September 15, 2011 9:36 AM
Subject: Re: Message

The point I was trying to make was that there's no job on the planet Earth that she won't decide to "hate." I know the grocery store isn't exactly fun, but it's one of the few low-stress jobs out there that she can actually handle (and it's not cleaning toilets, or waiting on tables, or scrubbing dishes, etc.). In other words, it's just about the best situation she could have found, given her mental health issues and drinking history. The only drawback is the lack of hours. So despite all of the positive aspects of the job, and the fact that it's a good fit for her (other than the hours), she is slowly but surely deciding to hate it. Like every other part of her life, Michelle seems to be looking for a way to blow-up the job, and self-destruct once again. The only message we can give her is, don't do it. She has very few (if any) options left in life. And I'm afraid that moving her to a nicer place or wherever else won't make her any less self-destructive. We know it won't stop her from drinking, and we know it won't make her stop hating any job she's lucky enough to have. So the only advice I can give her (which I will) is, stop hating the job, and start loving it. You have absolutely no other options.

From: Mary Greer
To: Tina Greer
Date: September 29, 2011 8:52 AM
Subject: Various

Hey, Tina,

Anyway, the school year seems to be off to a good start–we can talk more about that on the phone perhaps. Too soon to tell, but so far we are very impressed with Joni's new school. Jamie also seems much happier/mature this year. We'll see . . .

Michelle got fired, which is a major crisis . . . she is not doing well. She says it has nothing to do with drinking, but frankly I doubt that is true. Marc is still taking care of bills, etc. so it is not like she is going to be homeless for the short term, but this situation just can't continue. Not sure what is going to happen. Sigh . . .

Call me when you can . . . .

Love, Mary

From: Mary Greer
To: Marc Charles
Date: September 30, 2011 8:42 PM
Subject: Michelle

Are you online? Please call me!

From: Mary Greer
To: Marc Charles
Date: October 7, 2011 7:25 AM
Subject: Michelle's number

This is what she gave me: XXX-XXX-XXXX. Let me know when you talk to her, and what is happening/how she sounds.

From: Marc Charles
To: Mary Greer
Date: October 19, 2011 12:40 PM
Subject: Rez

Mary - The reservation will be at 5 pm on Saturday, not 4:30. For some reason they wouldn't take one earlier than 5.

From: Mary Greer
To: Marc Charles
Date: October 19, 2011 1:15 PM
Subject: Re: Rez

Ok, fine. I am sure the answer is no or you would have told me, but any word from Michelle? I am very, very worried about her now.

From: Marc Charles
To: Mary Greer
Date: October 20, 2011 9:00 AM
Subject: Re: Rez

I've left her messages every couple of days for about a week. I can see on-line that she withdrew $3400 from the IRA account yesterday, $1400 of which was immediately withheld for Federal and State taxes. She netted exactly $2000.

As usual, she is doing incredibly stupid things. I'll leave her a message, and tell her that she is now completely on her own. She can start paying her own rent, since she's foolishly decided to start drawing down on the only savings account she has.

From: Mary Greer
To: Marc Charles
Date: October 20, 2011 9:27 AM
Subject: Re: Rez

Can we talk? I think she is in trouble and perhaps we should approach this more as reducing her risk of harm to herself (called "harm reduction" now in substance abuse treatment) instead of punishment. Stopping her rent is just going to make things worse. Maybe we could go see her together? Maybe she would let us talk to her counselor?

From: Marc Charles
To: Mary Greer
Date: October 21, 2011 12:48 PM
Subject: Oct-21

Mary - I left Michelle another message today. I told her I saw the withdrawal, and that she should use it to start paying her rent again.

I also told her I would love to help her, but won't/can't do anything until she commits fully/enthusiastically to the Serenity program.

If she does call you, let me know right away. You should frankly just tell her to call me. I don't want the message we're giving her to be different from you than from me.

See you tomorrow at 5. Feel free to give me a call if need be.

From: Marc Charles
To: Mary Greer
Date: November 24, 2011 10:41 PM
Subject: Happy Thanksgiving

Hope the Greers had a great Thanksgiving today... We'll see you all next Friday night.

From: Mary Greer
To: Marc Charles
Date: November 25, 2011 9:29 AM
Subject: Re: Happy Thanksgiving

You, too! We did have a turkey and it was very nice, but our main Thanksgiving is that we are having "Dinner with the Pilgrims" on Saturday. We go there every year—it is great fun. Yesterday was just a little sad because last year we had Dad with us, Liam's dad was also here, and Michelle was here too.

We'll see you Friday, but I'll call you later this week to firm things up.

From: Marc Charles
To: Mary Greer
Date: December 13. 2011 10:13 AM
Subject: Sunday

Mary - How would you feel about Christine and I stopping by on Sunday afternoon (between 2 and 3) to give the kids their gifts and say hello? I'd like to do it before Christmas if we can . . . We don't need to stay too long if you guys are busy . . . On another note, how old is Peter now, 2? Have you heard about any gift ideas from Malcolm? Seth is only at 6 or 7 months, right? What do you get for a baby? Let me know if you have any ideas.

I checked the Fidelity website; Michelle did withdraw another $1500 from the IRA. Her "net" check after taxes withheld was only $1000. Otherwise, I haven't heard from her, and I won't call her unless she reaches out to discuss treatment.

Hope all is well with the Greers . . .

From: Marc Charles
To: Mary Greer
Date: December 26, 2011 9:40 AM
Subject: Hello

Mary - Got your message last night - Hope the Greers had a great Christmas. We still plan on coming down next Saturday to say Hi and give you your gifts. How about between 4 and 5? It will be New Year's Eve, so we don't want to be on the road too late. I got Jamie the Guggenheim Museum and the 30 Rockefeller Center LEGO kits. Does he already have one of these (or both)? If so, let me know and I'll pick up something else.

Take care . . .

From: Mary Greer
To: Marc Charles
Date: December 26, 2011 10:06 AM
Subject: Re: Hello

1) Yes, that would be great to see you early on New Year's Eve! Maybe we could go out to dinner at this really good Italian restaurant near us? Let me know and I will make a reservation–what time would you want?

2) Jamie has neither of those LEGO sets—thank you so much. He will love them. They are very expensive–you didn't need to get two. Were you able to find some perfume for Joni?

3) Did you hear from Michelle? I thought about her and Dad (and Mom and Nana . . .) all day. Was feeling a bit melancholy, actually, though we did have a very nice Christmas.

From: Marc Charles
To: Mary Greer
Date: December 26, 2011 3:06 PM
Subject: Re: Hello

Sounds fun - Have Christine and I been there before? I don't remember. We better say 5 pm to be safe. We did get a couple of gift perfume sets for Joni; they weren't expensive (neither were the LEGO kits really).

I sent Michelle a card for Christmas, but she shipped it back to me unopened (!) For all she knew there could have been cash in it (there wasn't, but ...). Her total withdrawals from the IRA account are still sitting at $4500 so far, but I'm betting that she'll ramp up the activity in 2012.

She really is a very, very strange individual. She pulls tantrums that cry out for help, but then refuses the help when it is offered. I wouldn't be too sad about it, as she really doesn't seem to want us to be involved in her life. She instead seems to be fixated on someone giving her money, and leaving her to spend it as she pleases.

Unfortunately, given her alcoholism and mental health issues, no one in the world is willing to do that without seeing her in a regimented/monitored treatment program, and she refuses to do that.

No one, therefore, can help her until she stops denying her problems and agrees to treatment. I think she knows that (she's certainly been told in no uncertain terms), and it makes her mad. So be it - when she's ready to start the program, I will help (and you can too). Until then, she needs to be strictly avoided. She is not well, and the only people who should be dealing with her at this point are mental health professionals and addiction specialists.

2012

From: Marc Charles
To: Mary Greer
Date: January 22, 2012 6:05 PM
Subject: Jan-22

Mary - Got your message. I'm not too worried about Michelle having the funds to fix her furnace, because she's withdrawn nearly $20,000 from her IRA account over the last three months or so. I would just leave her alone for now. She seems to want to do things her way, for better or worse.

From: Mary Greer
To: Marc Charles
Date: January 27, 2012 11:16 AM
Subject: Old Message

Marc,

I was looking thru my old calls looking for a phone number, and apparently Michelle tried to call me on Jan 20 at 3:20pm. She didn't leave a message, and I didn't even know she called. The number was her original cell number, so she still has it. I wonder what she wanted?

Mary

From: Marc Charles
To: Mary Greer
Date: January 27, 2012 11:55 AM
Subject: Re: Old Message

Well, if she wanted to have a rational, productive conversation I think she would have left you a message. My advice would be to continue to wait for her to do that. If she instead leaves you the same kind of ranting/bizarre messages she has in the past, then you should continue to steer clear from her. I don't think there's an easier answer here.

From: Mary Greer
To: Marc Charles
Date: October 15, 2012 8:19 AM
Subject: Call?

I see that you tried to call me at 7:30 this morning. Tried to call back but can't get thru. What's up?

From: Marc Charles
To: Mary Greer
Date: October 15, 2012 8:50 AM
Subject: Re: Call?

I was sitting on the train this morning and must have sat on an "auto-dial" number! Sorry about that. Two or three letters came in from Michelle over the last month or so (since I tried to talk to her in person a few weeks ago). All very similar - messy, illegible handwriting, railing against her landlord, her family, and the town, and nearly incoherent. Really nothing new, except her condition continues to deteriorate. I'll give you a call in a day or two to discuss . . .

2013

From: Marc Charles
To: Mary Greer
Date: April 19, 2013 11:45 AM
Subject: message

Hi Mary - Got your voicemail. I still have April 27th down for meeting up. Work has been shut down all day (all the trains too) so I'm just trying to work from home here. Hope all is well on the island.

From: Mary Greer
To: Marc Charles
Date: April 21, 2013 4:02 PM
Subject: Re: message

I can make a reservation–what time works for you? 6pm? Also, looking for advice–should I try to send a card to Michelle for her birthday?

From: Marc Charles
To: Mary Greer
Date: April 21, 2013 5:20 PM
Subject: Re: message

How about 5, to beat the crowds? I wouldn't give Michelle a chance to rant at this point. I'll give you a call during the week to discuss . . . Nothing is really new with Michelle; I just think she will use a harmless thing like a birthday card to lash out at people again (based on her track record).

From: Mary Greer
To: Marc Charles
Date: April 22, 2013 2:04 PM
Subject: Re: message

Understood. Sigh.

Also, I made a reservation for 5pm for this Saturday. We'll see you then. Looking forward to it.

Mary

From: Marc Charles
To: Mary Greer
Date: April 23, 2013 6:38 PM
Subject: Re: message

Thanks Mary. I'll try to call you this week to talk more about Michelle.

From: Marc Charles
To: Mary Greer
Date: July 22, 2013 7:15 PM
Subject: Re: Reunion

Thanks Mary. I heard from Michelle a couple of weeks ago but she hung up quickly when I started to talk about Serenity, treatment, etc.

2014

From: Marc Charles
To: Mary Greer
Date: November 28, 2014 12:43 AM
Subject: Nov. 27

Happy Thanksgiving Greers. Looking forward to seeing all of you on Dec. 13th.

From: Mary Greer
To: Marc Charles
Date: December 1, 2014 8:36 AM
Subject: Re: Nov. 27

Belated thanks . . . hope yours was good as well. Liam's dad has been here since last Monday (thru tomorrow)–very hectic.

Any word from Michelle?

2015

From: Marc Charles
To: Mary Greer, Malcolm Charles
Date: January 22, 2015 2:27 PM
Subject: ..

Got a call from the County constable an hour ago. Michelle will be evicted on Monday unless she pays the landlord $5k. She claims she has "some" of the money and will pay it by tomorrow. Landlord (I believe) still has right to evict even after partial payment. Things have come to a head and we may have to intervene.

From: Malcolm Charles
To: Marc Charles
Cc: Mary Greer
Date: January 22, 2015 2:44 PM
Subject: Re: ..

Thanks for the heads up. Could we talk about this by phone? I can conference both of you in using my iPhone. I'm going to be in the car for the next hour, so could speak now, and I'll be able to speak freely tonight after 8 PM.

From: Marc Charles
To: Malcolm Charles
Cc: Mary Greer
Date: January 22, 2015 2:47 PM
Subject: Re: ..

OK to call me now.

From: Mary Greer
To: Tina Greer
Date: January 27, 2015 11:17 AM
Subject: Re: Let it snow!

Hey, Tina,
Where are you? Can I call you? Very bad news about Michelle.

Mary

From: Marc Charles
To: Mary Greer
Date: February 5, 2015 2:41 PM
Subject: . . .

Yet another form to fill out. The case manager says they will need this form to pay for a skilled nursing facility for Michelle. We can fill it out, but Michelle needs to sign it. They won't accept photocopies, PDFs, etc. We can hammer it out together on a call if you like.

From: Marc Charles
To: Mary Greer
Date: February 5, 2015 3:23 PM
Subject: ..

Mary - Just FYI, the case manager recommended the HMO health plan option for Michelle, as she thinks it covers more providers on or near the island.

From: Mary Greer
To: Marc Charles
Date: February 5, 2015 3:52 PM
Subject: Re:..

Ok, but fat chance getting thru on the connecter phone line–what a nightmare. It is just as bad as I have read about in the papers. I just left a message for the lady in the Financial Office who helped me file the application to see if she can help sign her up. If not, I will try the phone line again tomorrow.

From: Marc Charles
To: Mary Greer
Date: February 5, 2015 5:43 PM
Subject: Re: ..

OK, thanks. I hope Michelle appreciates all this someday.

From: Mary Greer
To: Marc Charles
Date: February 6, 2015 9:15 AM
Subject: Application

1) She is enrolled, effective March 1. Until then, she just stays on the fee for service (the way she is now). They will send info confirming to the mailing address in 3-4 days; her member card will come 10-14 days after March 1. She will need to pick a primary care doctor–the available list will be in the materials they send, but we should probably ask the case manager who she should pick.

2) Let me know what time you want to go thru the disability application. I can do any time before 2–it will only take 10-15 minutes tops.

From: Marc Charles
To: Mary Greer
Date: February 6, 2015 12:26 PM
Subject: Re: Application

Thanks for getting this done Mary. I'm hoping to give you a call at 1:30.

From: Malcolm Charles
To: Marc Charles
Cc: Mary Greer
Date: February 12, 2015 6:23 PM
Subject: Michelle not transferred tonight

Marc,

I called Michelle at 6:10pm this evening just to check in, and she told me there was a "screw-up" and that she is not being transferred tonight.

When I called her, I was unaware anything was going on, I was just calling to say hello - as I tried to find out what was happening Michelle said she had two nurses waiting with her to take her to the bathroom, so I was rushed off the phone. She did mention that there was an ambulance driver there at some point but he was sent away, again because there seemed to be some mix-up. That is all the information I could get.

I wish I could tell you more. Let me know if you need me to do anything.

Malcolm

From: Mary Greer
To: Marc Charles
Date: February 16, 2015 8:00 AM
Subject: Phone, etc.

Marc,

A few updates:

1. I found a charger here that works on Michelle's phone and have got it working. I am going to try to drop it off later today. She has 4 hours of time left on it, so we might as well just keep that one going for now. I will let you know when she has it, so you will know that you can call her.

2. If Malcolm is going to start doing the insurance (which would be great), he should use your name since you are a designee. Otherwise, they won't talk to him. I have attached a scan of your form, so he has your information.

3. Regarding her primary care doc, I looked at the plan online and within that, there are 4 levels. I am pretty sure she will have the Network Together level, but as soon as you get her card in the mail you should be able to tell. Assuming that is what she will have, there are a lot of docs that take that insurance, according to the website anyway. But I was thinking you might ask Serenity when you talk to them if there are any doctors they particularly know around here who do well with substance abuse patients. For example, my primary is on the list and I know she

would have no clue what to do with someone like Michelle. So, maybe when you talk to Serenity about trying to get her on their waiting list you could also ask them about docs? Otherwise, we are really flying blind. If they do know someone, I think that no matter what hospital they are at, we should just go with that person if we can get them to accept Michelle as a patient.

4. I will call about her car insurance tomorrow.

That's it for now–will talk to you soon.

Mary

From: Mary Greer
To: Marc Charles
Date: February 17, 2015 10:06 AM
Subject: Car Insurance

Michelle's car insurance is a monthly $89.73, due on the 4th of each month. I just paid the late $89.73, which will keep her current till March 4. I put a note on my calendar on March 3 to decide if we want to pay that next monthly amount.

From: Marc Charles
To: Mary Greer
Date: February 17, 2015 4:10 PM
Subject: Re: Car Insurance

Thanks Mary. I can write you a check from the "Michelle" account this week. FYI her cell phone # is still XXX-XXX-XXXX. Not sure why she thought it had changed.

From: Mary Greer
To: Marc Charles
Date: February 17, 2015 5:26 PM
Subject: Re: Car Insurance

It's only 89 dollars. Don't worry about this one–if we keep it, then that account can start paying.

Did you talk to her? I am really worried about her edema. But on a more positive note, yesterday she seemed more concerned that they wouldn't let her stay (due to insurance) than complaining that she didn't like it. I think at this point she wants to be able to stay, which is good. And honestly, I can't figure out how they could let her go. Her legs are so big they are actually leaking. And she is definitely somewhat confused, which I read is also a symptom of cirrhosis because the toxins get into the brain. Regarding the phone, she was trying to tell me she had two phones and that this phone was the wrong phone—I couldn't figure out what she was talking about, but so long as she has a phone I am not going to worry about it.

From: Mary Greer
To: Tina Greer
Date: February 24, 2015 9:43 AM
Subject: News

Tina,

Michelle has been moved to a nursing home, but is in very, very bad shape. Would love to talk at some point. Very sad. Otherwise, we are all fine here, and think of you guys often!

Love, Mary

From: Mary Greer
To: Marc Charles
Date: February 25, 2015 12:07 PM
Subject: Mobile Home Insurance

Hi, Marc,

A quick update to let you know I was able to get thru to the mobile home insurance company. I paid the amount they said would enable us to keep the account current ($78.48), but they wouldn't give me any other information (I had to pay it blindly because they literally would not give me any info since I am not a designee; I only know the amount because it is showing up in my bank acct). They are sending a confirmation letter to her address, so it should get forwarded to you. From that letter, we should be able to see what is due next.

You mentioned you are starting to see hospital bills. Recall that the application was dated the day before she went in the hospital, (Jan. 25) so you might want to tell them to just resubmit. It should be covered.

And finally, I tried to call her with this tracphone, and she did call me back but I can't access the stupid voicemail until Jodi gets home. (It was her phone before we got her an iPhone so I don't have the password.) After I called Michelle last night, she left me three voicemails. Have you talked to her? Is everything all right? I have called her twice this morning and she has not answered.

Mary

From: Mary Greer
To: Marc Charles
Date: February 26, 2015 2:22 PM
Subject: Can you call me?

Marc,

Are you in Toronto? I am getting concerned because I have not been able to get thru to Michelle at all. You had said something about perhaps visiting her today (Thursday); is that still the plan?

I am going there on Saturday morning, but was hoping to start checking in daily with her by phone. If you talk to her, can you tell her to shut off going directly to voice mail and that XXX-XXX-XXXX is me?

Also, if you get a chance, please give me a call. I am wondering if we should start checking in with the nursing staff to get a true status update.

Mary

From: Marc Charles
To: Mary Greer
Date: February 26, 2015 4:26 PM
Subject: Re: Can you call me?

Turns out her phone is broken . . .

From: Mary Greer
To: Marc Charles
Date: February 26, 2015 4:33 PM
Subject: Re: Can you call me?

Ah, ok, maybe I can just give her this tracphone that I have. Don't say anything to her yet–let me talk to Liam.

From: Mary Greer
To: Marc Charles, Malcolm Charles
Date: February 28, 2015 11:31 AM
Subject: Michelle's New Telephone Number

Hi, guys,

I gave Michelle a replacement tracphone–her new telephone number is XXX-XXX-XXXX. For what it's worth, she said the best time for anyone to call is around suppertime.

Marc, I also dropped off some bigger clothes–she seemed to think they would work but is going to let me know after she tries them on.

Mary

From: Mary Greer
To: Tina Greer
Date: March 5, 2015 7:09 PM
Subject: Re: family vacation

Tina,

I can't believe we talked for almost two hours! Yikes! These pictures are beautiful–you should be a photographer, really!

Just got off the phone with Michelle–her ammonia levels have dropped to normal, which is very, very good news. I am so hoping things will turn around and maybe she can get that transplant . . . thanks for listening.

Will let you know when I choose a gift tomorrow.

From: Marc Charles
To: Mary Greer
Date: March 7, 2015 12:25 AM
Subject: Medicare Nursing Home Compare Results

Her nursing home scores highly in the official Medicare ratings as well. I'm thinking about sharing these printouts with Michelle.

From: Mary Greer
To: Marc Charles
Date: March 7, 2015 9:22 AM
Subject: Re: Medicare Nursing Home Compare Results

Thanks for this, and the other nursing home email you just sent. This is very helpful. At the Wednesday mtg–as you suggested–maybe we can get her back in the hospital (there is no question she needs more extensive medical attention right now) and then try for Pleasant Bay upon discharge. IF they will take her, that seems like the best option. We would just have to make her understand that no scenario is going to be perfect and she has to have realistic expectations.

BTW, the bottom of my car scraped on a mound of icy snow yesterday, and a big chunk of metal sheared off and is dragging on the ground. So, Liam is at the repair shop with it right now and I won't be able to see her today. She was not upset at all–she said she wanted to sleep anyway.

From: Mary Greer
To: Marc Charles
Date: March 8, 2015 12:45 PM
Subject: Michelle hospital?

Marc–have you heard anything else? I think I am going to run over to Community Hospital, but would like any info you have beforehand. Pls call me!

From: Mary Greer
To: Tina Greer
Cc: Liam Greer, Carl Morrison
Date: March 9, 2015 10:08 AM
Subject: Michelle

Tina and Carl,

Michelle passed away last night. Although we sort of expected it eventually, we certainly didn't expect it so fast. The nursing home transferred her to Community Hospital yesterday morning because she was vomiting blood–she spent the day in the ICU and then had some sort of major bleed into her abdomen and it was over within minutes. We can talk this weekend, but I wanted to let you know. I took the day off, but am off to the nursing home in a few minutes to pick up her things. I just want to get that part over with.

Love,

Mary

THE AFTERMATH

2015–2020

2015

From: Tina Greer
To: Mary Greer
Cc: Liam Greer, Carl Morrison
Date: March 9, 2015 1:50 PM
Subject: Re: Michelle

Dear Mary,

I am so sorry to hear this news. Please call if you want to talk or if there is anything that we can do. We send our love and prayers for you and everyone in the family.

I'm glad that you had a little time to be with Michelle while she was sober before she passed. That was a blessing!

Love,
Tina

From: Funeral Home
To: Marc Charles
Date: March 10, 2015 at 9:31 AM
Subject: Form

Marc,
Sorry, I forgot to attach the second form.

From: Marc Charles
To: Malcolm Charles, Mary Greer
Date: March 11, 2015 12:14 AM
Subject: Fwd: Form

Here's the second form that didn't reach you the first time.

From: Mary Greer
To: Malcolm Charles, Marc Charles
Date: March 11, 2015 12:14 AM
Subject: Fwd: Form

Marc and Malcolm,
1) Marc, I am really sorry, but the 2nd attachment still didn't "attach." It is pasting into the text of the email itself, but only part of the form, I think. Maybe you can send it to my other email?

2) Marc, what time do you want Liam to meet you at the storage facility on Friday? He has a dental appt at 9, so could get there by 11. If you wanted to do it earlier, that is fine, just let me know and we will reschedule the appt.

3) Malcolm, it just occurred to me that I may have been confused when I answered your question about the Mass. I had just assumed they would have a Mass said for her in her name, is that right? (i.e., there is no way I could get down there to attend in person, unfortunately).

Mary

From: Malcolm Charles
To: Mary Greer, Marc Charles
Date: March 11, 2015 4:39 PM
Subject: Michelle's music

Hi,

On Monday when I was home, I searched for a tape Michelle and I'd made at Delano Street of the song "Eva" that she sung. I didn't find it, but I found the cassette of the gig (which I'd forgotten about) that we played in 1990. It was you (Marc), her, me, and this flutist I knew; I think Michelle and you were living in Ocean City and I was in St. John.

Anyway, it's very folk-y, and a few songs are good, a few are cringeworthy, and I made MP3s of some of them. People actually applauded us. It was our first show and we didn't quite know what we were doing but played all the songs all the way through with minimal screw-ups. Do you want me to share these with you on Dropbox?

If this kind of thing is too soon, please tell me. I was thinking of ways Michelle contributed happiness in people's lives, and she told me once she was happy when we all lived in Ocean City - and this also is a kind of documentary accomplishment of what she wanted to do musically, at least in part. And Marc, am I correct in recalling that legendary grunge-folkie was on the bill or at least there that night, and did she ask Michelle to do something musically with her?

From: Marc Charles
To: Mary Greer
Cc: Malcolm Charles
Date: March 11, 2015 9:37 PM
Subject: Re: VARIOUS

It would be great if Liam could meet me right at 11am on Friday. I'll send the address tomorrow. Please remind him we aren't really going to clear anything out on Friday (except maybe a few boxes of documents and her computer, if we can find it). Malcolm, no need for you to be there on Friday, because we're not ready to do any real work just yet.

From: Marc Charles
To: Malcolm Charles
Cc: Mary Greer
Date: March 11, 2015 9:56 PM
Subject: Re: Michelle's music

Thanks, Malcolm. Eventually, it would be nice to have a CD of Michelle singing a few songs. I have a few cassettes I could also share with you if you have the hardware & software to convert them to CD. I do remember the "big debut" at the cafe. You're right, she was there and said something to Michelle about maybe working together (although she was admittedly kind of a ditz).

From: Marc Charles
To: Mary Greer
Date: March 12, 2015 12:46 AM
Subject: Fwd: VARIOUS

Mary - The storage company is located at 8 South St. They'll need some sort of ID for Michelle - we may not have the death certificate by then. Can Liam bring her driver's license and anything else we might use to prove that we are related to her? Thanks for your help.

From: Mary Greer
To: Marc Charles
Cc: Malcolm Charles
Date: March 12, 2015 8:44 AM
Subject: Re: Michelle's music

I remember that night—I was there, too. I would LOVE to have a CD with her voice. Thank you, Malcolm.

From: Marc Charles
To: Mary Greer
Date: March 13, 2015 12:05 AM
Subject: Storage

Mary - I talked to the storage place this afternoon. They said the charge (for now) would be about $200. If Liam is going to have Michelle's cash with him, we'll use that to pay. They will also need to see Michelle's driver's license (since we don't have a death certificate yet). I'll plan on being there at 11 tomorrow to meet Liam.

From: Mary Greer
To: Marc Charles
Date: March 13, 2015 8:01 AM
Subject: Re: Storage

Yes, the cash ($541) is attached to the driver's license with an elastic. It is in her purse, in the bag Liam is going to give you. Thanks for doing this . . . so painful.

From: Malcolm Charles
To: Mary Greer, Marc Charles
Date: March 13, 2015 9:16 AM
Subject: A couple things

Hi,

I feel uneasy about the lack of a funeral and an obituary for Michelle. I raise this not to make a stink but because I worry down the road we may regret not doing either.

Re: the obit, I understand we don't want creditors and slimeballs crawling out of the woodwork, but her death will be a matter of public record. Also, I don't think one of Michelle's creditors would have a legal leg to stand on were they to try to come after us. I can ask a lawyer if that would make you feel comfortable. To be clear, I won't do anything unilaterally without both of you agreeing, but at least I would like to discuss this more.

As to a religious ceremony for Michelle, I don't know what you both have in mind or if she stated her wishes, and I don't recall her views on the Catholic church, but I do think we should have some kind of ceremony for her in the nearer term beyond casting her ashes in the canal - and while I was present for Dad's viewing, I wasn't present for Dad's burial, so I don't know what kind of religious ceremony or prayers were said graveside. If anyone knows what she thinks of the church, that'd be helpful, but if this is unclear, I'd be happy to reach out, for example, to the local

Unitarian church (which has probably the broadest view within Christianity as a way to accommodate Michelle's views) to arrange something. Again, I won't act unilaterally until I get your input, but Mom at least had a Mass and a burial, and it just depresses me to think Michelle won't be memorialized similarly.

Again, your thoughts are welcome, because I don't quite know what you want to do and what you have planned.

Malcolm

From: Mary Greer
To: Malcolm Charles
Cc: Marc Charles
Date: March 13, 2015 9:52 AM
Subject: Re: A couple things

Let's do this by conference call.

From: Malcolm Charles
To: Mary Greer
Cc: Marc Charles
Date: March 13, 2015 12:06 PM
Subject: Re: A couple things

Sure, just let me know what day/time may work for you both.

From: Marc Charles
To: Malcolm Charles
Cc: Mary Greer
Date: March 14, 2015 12:22 AM
Subject: Re: A couple things

I'm fine with a memorial service for immediate family at either a church or the funeral home. I'm still very opposed to publishing an obituary, and it has nothing to do with creditors. The people that need to (or even deserve to) know about her death already know about it. People like Jackson, the landlord who evicted her, the Mendoza guy who stole $10k from her, Tommy Gleason, etc. have no business being privy to this news. The only other people (besides us) who might want to formally acknowledge her death would be Noreen and Leah, but even that's a long shot, and we could simply send them a note informing them of what happened if we feel it's important that they know. I just think it's time to leave her in peace, without providing any clues to the outside world about how difficult the last few years have been for her. Her suffering is nobody else's business is another way of putting it, I guess.

From: Mary Greer
To: Marc Charles
Cc: Malcolm Charles
Date: March 14, 2015 9:16 AM
Subject: Re: A couple things

Malcolm, I hear your concerns, respect them, and love you for it. However, I too am completely opposed to the obituary. These people are actually dangerous. Michelle told me that Mendoza was a registered sex offender, and the landlord's people threatened her–that is why she had those boards over her windows. The island is a small community–everybody knows everyone's business–I live here and my kids live here. I do not want to be connected to this in any way. Period.

Regarding notifying anyone, I don't even know where Noreen and Leah live anymore, and don't think we should even try to reconnect. Michelle had no contact really with anyone in years–and no one cared enough to try to contact her either–so as you say, Marc, anyone who needs to know already does.

And I am also open to a memorial service, but totally private–just our three families. Malcolm, as I told Marc, the Greers are the nicest people you will ever meet and they never did an obituary or a service for Sarah. It is just not something that they do. In fact, her ashes are still sitting in Harry's bedroom. Michelle was, to say the least, not religious, and left no wishes whatsoever that I know of. But if you wanted to do something now, we should talk by phone today or tomorrow. We can also do something later, but we should make a decision.

I hate doing this over email. Can we set up 15 minutes today or tomorrow for a group call just to settle on what, if anything, we want to do for a service? And if so, when?

Love, Mary

From: Marc Charles
To: Mary Greer
Cc: Malcolm Charles
Date: March 14, 2015 1:03 PM
Subject: Re: A couple things

Let's talk on the phone on Monday. It's hard for me to focus on anything with the baby running around on weekends. I'll try to send some times tomorrow. Malcolm, can you do FaceTime at 6:30 tonight, so I can thank everyone for the gift card?

From: Malcolm Charles
To: Marc Charles
Cc: Mary Greer
Date: March 14, 2015 4:01 PM
Subject: Re: A couple things

Marc: yes, let's facetime at 6:30 tonight.

I want to clarify something: first, I am not looking to make a stink, I just want to repeat that. And to be clear, the idea for an obituary is not to share information about Michelle's death, but instead as a way to show her mark on the world, as I think any human being would want to, and as a demonstration of our love for her. That is, it could mention her love of music, her love of animals, perhaps the year she graduated from college. And we could say she died after either a brief or a long illness.

And to be more clear, we don't need to list our names in terms of who survives her; we could easily say she is survived by her siblings, and her nephews and nieces.

And to be very, very clear: for a memorial, like you I do not want certain people showing up. So I would not want to list funeral or memorial information in an obit.

Anyway, yes, let's talk on the phone on Monday, and I appreciate you hearing me out. Marc, I'm sure like you, I do not want to bring up any of this during the facetime tonight.

Best,
Malcolm

From: Mary Greer
To: Malcolm Charles
Cc: Marc Charles
Date: March 18, 2015 6:59 PM
Subject: Re: What we discussed on conf. call

Answers below each section.

From: Malcolm Charles
To: Marc Charles, Mary Greer
Date: March 18, 2015 5:56 PM
Subject: What we discussed on conf. call

Memorial: As much as I'd like Kate and the kids to come up (the kids wouldn't go to the wake) I'm going to need to come solo if we want to do this any time before May. It's logistically very difficult for all of us to be there and tough on the kids, even though Kate would like to pay her respects because she did hang out with Michelle quite a bit. So, if you could remind me of the two dates (one in March, one in April, I think) I can make that work, but it'll be just me. A Saturday for one of these dates would be best, if at all possible. A wake at a funeral home or whatever with a minister of some sort, and casting her ashes in the canal, is all fine with me.

I seem to recall with Dad's that they only did these Monday through Friday, but will let Marc ring in here.

Headstone: I think we should have one for her. Also, Kate mentioned that a colleague of hers had someone plant a tree for her recently deceased father, with a plaque at the foot of it. Perhaps we could do this either as an alternative or in addition to a headstone?

I am fine with whatever you decide.

Trailer: I don't want to pursue this. It seems like the landlord would attempt to recoup his costs, and I imagine the trailer is in poor shape. If she has any other outstanding claims or debts, setting up an estate for her seems like a bad idea to me. So, my vote is "no" on this one.

OK, agree.

Obit: As I said, I only want to move forward if there is full consensus. With that, on the one hand I think it's natural to not want certain people to read an obit in the paper or online and then think they can come after you somehow. However, what I'm proposing is no one's name but hers will be in the obit, with a generic reference to nieces and nephews. Our names wouldn't be in it. To put it plainly - and I'm sorry to write this vs. speak it directly, but it's taken me 36-48 hours to formulate my thoughts and I figure this will save the time of arranging another conf. call between us - I think foregoing an obit for the reasons you both described is part of a pattern of alcoholic behavior our family has suffered, endured, and enacted for decades. There is no shame for us that she drank herself to death. Mary, you yourself said on the phone there was nothing we could do to stop or save her. While I can't predict the future, I think it's safe to say no one will come to your door or email or call you about an obit that doesn't even mention who her family was. This just strikes me as sweeping Michelle under the rug, as some kind of human embarrassment we should take pains and great haste to forget. I'm sad for her, but I'm not embarrassed and do not care what anyone thinks at my work, in my community, etc. If someone tries to show up at my door or call me, I will call the cops. Related, no obit basically means her life, who she was, is wiped away, erased - like she never existed. She did live a life with some meaning and even some happiness, at least up to her 30s. The three of us are her only advocates now. I of course realize she didn't want us to be advocates when she was alive and drinking, and she's dead now so it's easy to say, so what? Let's just move on. Even though she's dead, I would like to do what I think she would have expressed her "last wishes" to be when she was alive and still vital, not in the throes of her mental illness and alcoholism. Again, I'm not trying to pick a fight or create some quixotic "cause" about this as a reaction to her death, nor will I press the point if you are unpersuaded. But I think it's pretty lousy we're not giving her an obit, and I do wish you would reconsider.

Liam and I both strongly do not want an obit for all the reasons I have already said. This is not alcoholic-family behavior. These are bad people—Mendoza is in jail and the landlord is not much better. She has left a lot of loose ends and I have no idea where all her court cases stand. And they do know who her family members are.

If you think it's a good idea, I will look into getting her a tree and a plaque somewhere. I have to look into how this works, though, but I imagine it's pretty straightforward.

OK.

Thanks for listening/reading.

Malcolm

From: Marc Charles
To: Malcolm Charles, Mary Greer
Date: March 21, 2015 12:16 AM
Subject: ..

How do you both feel about Sat-Apr-18th for the memorial service, at around 2pm? The funeral home has a room available. Maybe we could get some pictures uploaded for their digital monitor, and play a few recordings of Michelle singing.

From: Mary Greer
To: Marc Charles
Cc: Malcolm Charles
Date: March 21, 2015 11:58 AM
Subject: Re: ..

April 18 at 2pm is fine with us. Maybe we could also plan to all have dinner together after?

From: Malcolm Charles
To: Mary Greer
Cc: Marc Charles
Date: March 21, 2015 2:12 PM
Subject: Re: ..

That works, but it will just be me.

From: Mary Greer
To: Malcolm Charles
Date: March 21, 2015 2:47 PM
Subject: Re: ..

Are you planning to stay overnight? Do you want to sleep here before heading back on Sunday?

From: Marc Charles
To: Mary Greer
Date: March 22, 2015 11:48 PM
Subject: ..

Mary - Any good birthday gift ideas for the kids this year? Also, I got a reminder postcard in the mail from Michelle's vet that said Scooter's 3-year vaccinations for distemper and rabies are due next month. I know you said you already brought him to the vet a few weeks ago; maybe these shots were already covered. Just letting you know.

From: Mary Greer
To: Marc Charles
Date: March 23, 2015 9:14 AM
Subject: Re: ..

Hi Marc,

For the kids, I know they would love Amazon gift cards. They really like being able to go online and "shop."

And on Scooter, yes, I had already had them all re-done, but good to know she was keeping up with it. He is astonishingly old (15!) and the vet said he is in great shape considering his age.

Mary

From: Marc Charles
To: Malcolm Charles, Mary Greer
Date: March 26, 2015 12:53 AM
Subject: Service

Is it ok to lock in Sat-Apr-18 at 2 pm for Michelle's service? The funeral home is bugging me to make a decision. I also need them to line up a priest.

Can we collect whatever photos we have of Michelle and get them scanned onto a CD so we can show them on the video screen during the service?

Malcolm, you can stay with us on Saturday night if you like.

From: Mary Greer
To: Marc Charles
Cc: Malcolm Charles
Date: March 26, 2015 6:26 AM
Subject: Re: Service

Marc,

Yes, that is fine–I do already have that on my calendar.

Mary

From: Malcolm Charles
To: Mary Greer, Marc Charles
Date: March 26, 2015 12:16 PM
Subject: Re: Service

Yes, that's fine.

Malcolm

From: Marc Charles
To: Malcolm Charles
Cc: Mary Greer
Date: March 26, 2015 5:15 PM
Subject: Re: Service

OK, I'll lock it in. Do we have a volunteer to scan some photographs if I mail them to you? Malcolm, if you're feeling ambitious, I could send you 5 or 6 home recordings of Michelle singing some songs that she liked (also to be scanned to CD).

Malcolm - Should Christine and I plan on you coming back with us afterwards?

Finally, weather permitting, I'd like to suggest we scatter the ashes in the canal immediately after the service. It's right near the funeral home, and who knows when we'll all be gathered together in one place. We can still go out for dinner afterwards if people are up for it. Please let me know what you think.

From: Malcolm Charles
To: Marc Charles
Cc: Mary Greer
Date: March 26, 2015 5:17 PM
Subject: Re: Service

Yes, I've been horribly lax scanning family photos so I can scan those and the ones of Michelle I have now, and upload them to Dropbox. I can convert cassettes and CDs to MP3, as well.

I don't know what my plans are exactly but I will let you know asap.

Malcolm

From: Marc Charles
To: Malcolm Charles
Cc: Mary Greer
Date: March 26, 2015 5:44 PM
Subject: Re: Service

Thanks Malcolm. Your effort will help make this a very nice service. I'll try to FedEx some pictures etc. to you as soon as I can.

From: Mary Greer
To: Malcolm Charles
Cc: Marc Charles
Date: March 28, 2015 2:18 PM
Subject: Re: Service

Hi, Malcolm,

Two things:
1) We sent a gift for Peter's birthday–it should arrive (hopefully) by the end of the week.
2) I am going to put about 20 pictures into FedEx on Monday. I don't have many pictures, unfortunately. (I do not know what happened to all those childhood family albums.)

Anyway, thanks for doing the scanning.

Mary

From: Mary Greer
To: Marc Charles
Date: April 4, 2015 12:40 PM
Subject: Flowers

Do you want to talk about that this weekend?

Or do you just want to give me a dollar amount and I will go with what the florist recommends?

From: Marc Charles
To: Mary Greer
Date: April 6, 2015 5:58 PM
Subject: Re: RESEND: Flowers

I think we're just going to have a setup like we did for Dad, like a framed picture on a stand with a flower arrangement on either side of it. I have no idea what that would cost, but if it's a few hundred dollars I think we should spend the money out of Michelle's final arrangements budget, as it seems like the right thing to do. I'll send you a check if you want to get an estimate from a local place.

From: Mary Greer
To: Marc Charles
Date: April 7, 2015 9:57 AM
Subject: Re: RESEND: Flowers

Marc,
How about 2 of these? They are 175 each, so it would be 350 plus tax and delivery. The link defaults to the home page, so go to the sympathy menu, and just scroll to for the service, and then to the wreath (which is on a stand, so I think it would work).

And also, do you have a framed picture you are planning to bring, or is Malcolm having one made? I don't have anything here . . . and since I sent Malcolm all my good pictures, I literally have nothing I could use to have one made.

Mary

From: Marc Charles
To: Mary Greer
Date: April 7, 2015 11:18 AM
Subject: Re: RESEND: Flowers

That looks nice - Please feel free to order them. I'll get you a check. Good point on the framed picture; Malcolm has everything right now. I'll tell him to get it all scanned so we can pick out the best one, and then I'm sure it can be blown up to an 8x10 or so on an iPad. Christine has a color printer for photos; I can put it in a frame.

From: Mary Greer
To: Marc Charles
Date: April 8, 2015 11:04 AM
Subject: Re: RESEND: Flowers

Ok, the order is all set. They will call the funeral home the day before to arrange delivery for April 18. They have the stands, she said.

Total cost came to $379.35. I put it on our credit card–just send a check when you can.

From: Marc Charles
To: Mary Greer
Date: April 10, 2015 5:52 PM
Subject: Re: RESEND: Flowers

Ok, thanks, will get a check out this weekend. Did the woman from the funeral home contact you about Michelle yet? Bad news on our babysitting front; we can't get someone we trust to cover the 6+ hours we need on the 18th so Christine's going to have to stay home with the baby. If nothing else this means I won't need to rush through the service, the canal, dinner, etc. on Saturday.

From: Mary Greer
To: Marc Charles
Date: April 11, 2015 12:57 PM
Subject: Re: RESEND: Flowers

I can see why Christine wouldn't want to leave the baby for so long–that's fine.

And yes, I did speak to the woman from the funeral home.

From: Malcolm Charles
To: Mary Greer, Marc Charles
Date: April 12, 2015 9:28 PM
Subject: Image for 8x11 print

Please take a look at the attached PDF – there aren't many pictures to choose from of Michelle as an adult, and we need an 8 x 11 print for the memorial. (In addition to the other photo scans I will have ready likely by Wednesday.) So, of the three attached, please let me know which one you think is best. Otherwise, we would have to go for something from her childhood.

Thanks,
Malcolm

From: Marc Charles
To: Malcolm Charles
Cc: Mary Greer
Date: April 12, 2015 11:17 PM
Subject: Re: Image for 8x11 print

Thanks Malcolm - I like the first one the best (Michelle with short hair & big earrings), but think they all would work. Maybe we'll frame a couple of them for the service.

From: Mary Greer
To: Marc Charles
Cc: Malcolm Charles
Date: April 13, 2015 9:43 AM
Subject: Re: Image for 8x11 print

I, too, love the one with the big earrings. Wow, so beautiful ... But a couple might be nice. Dad had two at his service. The one with the red dress is nice–Malcolm, that was actually taken at your college graduation.

From: Malcolm Charles
To: Mary Greer
Date: April 13, 2015 10:02 AM
Subject: Re: Image for 8x11 print

I will scan them (and the other Michelle photos) as high res as possible - just recall these are not "portrait" images (except for her graduation photo), but standard issue late-80s/early-90s camera shots. So, I'm not sure how well they'll enlarge to 8x11, however high res I make them. Any marks or scratches will also enlarge, too, which hopefully I can fix in photoshop. Just setting expectations. Of all the images I have in that box of photo albums, there are precious few of Michelle as a post-college adult. Anyway, I'll send you a link to Dropbox in the next night or two, wherein you can choose all the images of Michelle you want. Some of her solo, most with family, etc.

From: Marc Charles
To: Mary Greer
Cc: Malcolm Charles
Date: April 13, 2015 10:42 AM
Subject: Re: Image for 8x11 print

Ok, I'll put them both in frames.

From: Marc Charles
To: Malcolm Charles
Cc: Mary Greer
Date: April 13, 2015 5:39 PM
Subject: Fwd: Re: Image for 8x11 print

Just FYI, the funeral home director says he has a Bluetooth speaker that can attach to an iPad or iPhone if that's how we plan on running our photos or slide show through their video set-up. I assume that means that whatever songs we want to play in conjunction with the photos need to be synced into the slide show right on the iPad, but my tech knowledge is obviously pretty weak. In any event he says he'll try to work with us regardless of whatever configuration we show up with.

From: Malcolm Charles
To: Marc Charles
Cc: Mary Greer
Date: April 13, 2015 5:46 PM
Subject: Re: Image for 8x11 print

OK, let me see what I can do in iMovie. I can test it on my Bluetooth speaker at home.

From: Marc Charles
To: Malcolm Charles
Cc: Mary Greer
Date: April 13, 2015 5:49 PM
Subject: Re: Image for 8x11 print

Ok, thanks Malcolm.

From: Malcolm Charles
To: Marc Charles
Cc: Mary Greer
Date: April 14, 2015 1:01 AM
Subject: Photos on Dropbox

Let me know if you can access the Dropbox link I sent.

Having spent some hours with the photos, what strikes me is how much Michelle smiled in so many photos from her toddler-hood up to her young adulthood in the 1980s (I don't have many other images after that, just a couple you sent me).

It's very sweet looking at the photos of her as a child, and as a young adult, and it reminds me how we were once a family that lived together, did things together, loved each other, etc. We picnicked, even! Went on vacations together, and all seemed to enjoy it!

But it broke all apart, dysfunction robbed us of each other and our family unit. And thus it's also heartbreaking to see these. Our parents ruined her, basically, and she never recovered from that, and kept going to people and things that hurt her. I was thinking that the only person who may have helped Michelle hold it together was Nana; maybe I'm wrong about that, but things went downhill for her shortly after that.

Anyway, seeing all these happy images reminds me of how much I loved her and love her, and how much I missed her as she fell apart and isolated herself, and I isolated Michelle from me, and how much I miss her now. I wish I could do something, pray or who knows what, to bring her back, but my hope is that she's at peace now and as I said before, I hope and pray Nana has welcomed her and is comforting her now and always. And perhaps the riddle of Mom and Dad and Michelle is solved in Heaven, and all is reconciled.

Malcolm

From: Marc Charles
To: Malcolm Charles
Cc: Mary Greer
Date: April 14, 2015 1:26 AM
Subject: Re: Photos on Dropbox

The slideshow is fantastic; thanks Malcolm. It's impossible not to shed some tears when you look at it. To your point below, I'm sure Michelle is at peace now. She had 30+ wonderful years on this planet, and then about 20 that no person should have to endure. I'm grateful for the good years we all had with her, and that she was always there to help us, and that once in a while we were able to help her too. I'm glad she was finally able to reach out to all of us a few months ago to reconnect when the rest of the world had let her down. In her own way I think that meant quite a lot to her. Mary was even able to see her on the very last day to remind her that we were with her, and that we cared. That's kind of a big deal, because Mom didn't have that, and many other people who suffer from alcoholism don't either. She was a good sister, she helped shape who each of us became, and she will be missed.

From: Mary Greer
To: Marc Charles
Cc: Malcolm Charles
Date: April 14, 2015 9:46 AM
Subject: Re: Photos on Dropbox

Thanks, Malcolm, the photos are so great. On the 8x11s, maybe just do all four?

Regarding the stream below . . . with me anyway, Michelle did not do a lot of deep emotional "processing" during the last 6 weeks of her life (it was mostly medical/practical conversations), but she most definitely was happy to have us back in her life. She said something like "thank God" I was nearby and a bunch of stuff like that. She knew she was not alone, that she was going to have help, and she even knew the nursing home coverage had been approved and that we were going to be finding her a new and better place.

Malcolm, it is also important that you know that she was not mad at Mom and Dad at the end. At the nursing home, she told me she wished she had her parents to help her through this illness, and she also dreamed about Dad and

Wolfie. She said it was an incredibly real and very good dream. I would like to think they were getting ready to welcome her to heaven (seriously). Her major regret was Nicholas–on her last day in the ICU at Community Hospital she said she wished she had married a good man, but that she didn't, and she wished she had had a family. I say this not to make anyone sad (keep in mind that same afternoon she also said kids were the kiss of death and also said the only reason I was telling her I loved her was because I thought she was dying)–but I do think she never got over her divorce. She came out of that marriage a completely different person from the one that went in.

From: Malcolm Charles
To: Mary Greer, Marc Charles
Date: April 14, 2015 12:03 PM
Subject: Re: Photos on Dropbox

Thanks. I wish I had more photoshop skill than I do (I tried to lighten/brighten a couple of the "portraits") but if nothing else these are how the photos actually appear. I would test print a few of these images at 8x11 and maybe somewhat smaller to see how they actually look. Also, I have probably another 50-100 to go through of her tonight, so I'll send you an updated link to those folders on Dropbox. This may motivate me to finish the rest - while there are a lot of albums, a lot of pics are missing. It's like an office building with half the windows knocked out.

Anyway, that's nice to hear, Mary, and I'm truly grateful you were there with her at the end, and you, too, Marc. In the '90s Michelle said to me in an episode of great unhappiness that she married Nicholas because she didn't want to be alone, which is heartbreaking in and of itself, and honestly I think she chose that sociopath because he replicated and perpetuated the abusive behavior she had been socialized with, sadly and in the end most tragically. I really do think - and this is totally unrealistic - her decline wouldn't have happened or would've been staved off had Nana lived into her 90s. I'm glad she wasn't mad at Mom and Dad, though obviously Mom's disease made her frankly unapproachable and unaffectionate - at least, that's my perception - and Michelle I think needed Nana's unconditional love and ability to stay pleasant and calm and warmly affirming no matter what calamity was befalling any/all of us. I know she mentioned to me her devastation that Nana was gone in her life.

And again, it's nice Mary to hear Michelle say she wished our parents were there with her, and I feel like a f-ing useless sh-t for not visiting her before it was too late, but I am still enraged at Mom and Dad for f-ing up her life so badly. When I was a kid, I was playing near our house toward the end of the street, and I saw Michelle walk up and asked her where she was going, I think she was a young teen then, and she gave some evasive answer I don't exactly recall, but I believe that's the same day she ran away. And I recall - perhaps inaccurately - that whoever she ran away with, that kid's mom and dad showed up for her at the shelter or wherever they were, but our Dad didn't, just Mom went to get her. Now, perhaps I'm inventing or misremembering this, but the kind of sh-tty behavior that led to her running away, and the other sh-tty behavior perpetuated for years on end by our parents' behavior and personal choices, and then by Michelle herself choosing Nicholas and succumbing to her disease and mental illness, put her in the ground last March. It is so sad I can't even express it.

I mention this I suppose to express and process my feelings, but also to say she was amazing for surviving as long as she did as a sane, functioning person. Scanning all these pictures I see my kids' faces in hers and yours as little kids, and I wonder how anyone could f- up so badly with their own children, and this is coming from me of all people.

But as you say, it was a gift to have Michelle with some of her family and to be as lucid as she could be, back to the real Michelle, even briefly, before she died.

From: Malcolm Charles
To: Mary Greer
Date: April 14, 2015 11:18 PM
Subject: Malcolm Charles shared "Michelle photos" with you

Here are about 50 or so more photos (despite the way I named them, they dropped in here and there, not as I'd hoped.) Anyway, please take a look. I also added Michelle's high school graduation photo as a possible portrait.

A couple things: is the photo "Michelle baby" actually Mom and Michelle? It's hard to say for me. Also, so sweet and heartbreaking to me, is the picture Michelle baby-toddler 19d, where she's holding in her right hand what's left of a lollipop on a stick.

Anyway, I'll pare these back for the slide show.

From: Marc Charles
To: Malcolm Charles, Mary Greer
Date: April 14, 2015 11:21 PM
Subject: Re: Malcolm Charles shared "Michelle photos" with you

I thought some of these pictures had been lost years ago. Thanks for putting this together; it's really great seeing all the memories in one place.

From: Mary Greer
To: Marc Charles
Cc: Malcolm Charles
Date: April 15, 2015 2:34 PM
Subject: Re: Malcolm Charles shared "Michelle photos" with you

Malcolm,

Regarding your message about the final slide show, my vote would be for random, but I am totally fine with whatever you and Marc want. It is so wonderful–thank you for doing it. If I wanted to save these pics, do I need to open and save them onto my computer one by one?

For what it's worth, the picture of Mom in the white dress with me and Michelle in the little green pants with the floral tops (toddler 4c) is actually of Michelle's first steps. That is why Dad took that shot.

And for me, the absolute most heartbreaking one is 4i.

Love, Mary

From: Mary Greer
To: Marc Charles
Date: April 17, 2015 9:15 AM
Subject: Car

Hi, Marc,

Since you are coming down here tomorrow anyway, I thought I would ask if you have the title to Michelle's car. I think I will need that, as well as a copy of her death certificate, to try to get the junk person to come and take it. If not, that's ok—we can wait till you have time to look for it. I just figured it was worth asking. I very much want to get that taken care of, since it is a painful reminder for all of us since it is sitting right in front of the house.

Do you know the situation with Malcolm for tomorrow yet? Should I try to make a reservation to eat somewhere? I just need to clue the kids in on what is happening–this is a pretty big thing in their lives.

Mary

From: Malcolm Charles
To: Mary Greer. Marc Charles
Date: April 17, 2015 3:33 PM
Subject: Malcolm Charles shared "Michelle EQed MP3s" with you

Here are the MP3s I EQ'ed (and added some trimming up front of count-ins, and fade-outs at the end). For the slide show - which I am frantically trying to export but it's a huge file - I have Eva as the first song and Candle Store as the second, followed by Baby Can I Hold You. I'd add "Baby . . . " second but it says "forgive me" and "sorry" over and over again, which is a big downer.

But, if you don't want Eva first, just let me know. I just figured she loved Nana, and she's singing it, and it's about the pain of someone you love dying, so . . . Anyway, let me know what you think. You should be able to right-click or whatever on each file and listen to them on your computer.

From: Mary Greer
To: Marc Charles, Malcolm Charles
Date: April 18, 2015 6:17 PM
Subject: Fwd:

Malcolm and Marc,

As promised, attached is Michelle's resume from January of 2010.

Love you guys . . . Mary

Michelle M. Jackson

Employment

Editorial Consultant 1993–present

Clients:
Allerton Publishing, Inc.
Torrence Corporation
Publica Publishing, Inc.
Sigma Investments
Group Motors
Blackenship Publishers, Inc.
Lee-Connor Publishing, Inc.
International Publishing, Inc.
Paul Riley, Inc.
State Highway Department
University of Technology

Transnational Translations, Inc.
Manager of Technical Documentation

DocuWrite Co.
Technical Writer and Editor

Century Publishing Company, Inc.
Technical Writer and Editor

Regis Software
Technical Editor

Jones and Lyons
Legal Proofreader and Copy Editor

Stanton State College
Library Assistant

Education
Stanton State College   B.A., English *(cum laude)*

North University   Paralegal Certificate

Other
Court-Appointed Special Advocate (CASA)
Provided pro bono supplementary court appearances with respect to children placed in foster care.

Michelle–Memorial Service April 18, 2015

The relationship of siblings is both simple and complex. You share a roof, sometimes a room or even a bed. You grow up as close as twins or can be separated by time, space and circumstance. No matter what the family configuration, there is something completely unique about sisters and brothers. You know the deepest secrets that you promised not to tell, and you share a heart that hurts when the other has troubles or struggles. They can be a pain and a delight. They can be brutally honest or blindly loyal. Your siblings are supposed to be there forever, to grow up and grow old with you. They see the world with you and help you make sense of the good, the bad and the ugly.

Michelle began her life in 1961. This was the year that the movies *West Side Story* and *The Absent-Minded Professor* premiered. Virgil Grissom became the second American astronaut to make a 118-mile-high, 303-mile-long rocket flight over the Atlantic. The Beatles performed in Liverpool for the first time. A gallon of gas was 25 cents and the average income was $5315.00.

Richard and Ann Charles brought that little baby girl home where she joined big sister Mary and those sisters were a tight-knit duo from the beginning. They loved spending weekends at Nana's and Mary recalled a time when Michelle got into some poison ivy and her eyes swelled shut. Michelle was sent to Nana's to recover where she was SPOILED (ALL capital letters). Mary shared that she was a little jealous that Michelle got to spend all that time alone with Nana even if it was because her eyes were swollen shut!

Those two sisters were joined by two little brothers, Marc and Malcolm, over the next 6 years. As a complete family of 6, they enjoyed family vacations at amusement parks. There were many fun family times at the cottage, the beaches and the island, playing in the yard, boating and exploring the woods near their childhood house.

Mary and Michelle shared so much as sisters. They rode the school bus together and were on the cheerleading squad at the same time. They even worked together doing laundry for 3 long years at the State School. They hated it with a passion but wanted to make some money so they sucked it up and did it together.

Michelle was funny, smart and beautiful. She was on the Prom Queen Court her Junior year of high school. She was very social and had lots of friends. She was dramatic and quick witted.

Malcolm recalled a time when his two sisters recorded commercials on a cassette recorder. Do you remember that, Mary? Michelle also had a love for music and Malcolm remembered all of you listening to albums on the stereo.

She loved to read and enjoyed learning. After graduating from Stanton High School, Michelle went on to State

University and studied drama. While there, she was the only freshman chosen to be in the college's play production. She then received her B.A. in English at Stanton State. Malcolm said he remembers when Michelle would come home from college with the wackiest hairstyles. The super-perm fro is forever engrained in his memory.

Michelle's love for learning continued and she began the Master's Program in Early Childhood Education at Stanton State. Later she earned her Paralegal Certificate at North University.

When Michelle got married, she and Nicholas spent a LOT of time with Mary and Liam. They loved sailing and eating Mexican food together. Mary and Michelle were very close and talked nearly every day. What great memories!

When Marc, Malcolm and Michelle all lived around the Ocean City area, their mutual love for music turned into a "band." Michelle sang, Marc played the guitar and bass and Malcolm was on the drums. Looking back on that time, both Malcolm and Marc quoted Michelle as saying that those "were the happiest times of my life."

Michelle was tender hearted and kind. This was exemplified more than once when, individually, Marc and Malcolm were in need of a place to stay. Michelle didn't hesitate but took in her little brothers for as long as they needed.

In January, Michelle reached out for help. That beautiful, smart, soft-hearted sister of yours was in a situation that she desired to re-connect. Did she know she was near the end of her life? Perhaps. You shared that those last 2½ months were not all butterflies and daisies. It was HARD, terrifying and painful, but yet you were thankful for that time and the chance to be with her.

That day came as a shock. No one expected March 8, 2015 to be Michelle's last day on Earth. Her struggle is finally over and she has found the peace that eluded her.

And left behind are you, her family, who have a hole in your hearts the size of Michelle. Though the end left you with a feeling of incompleteness and loss, the answer to finding your way on your grief journey will be to understand that sometimes you have to grieve that which you never had, that which you wish you had had. Grieving those rich years that you shared while grieving the promise and possibility that was never realized. Learning to live without Michelle means that you will miss her voice, her laugh, that quick wit, her tender heart . . . . You will miss your sister.

Every life is special; every life has a purpose and meaning. Every life is to be protected and celebrated. It is an important day when we stop to remember, to reflect and to remind ourselves of the unique and special person who was part of our lives. The journey of grief is a long and winding path and it is best walked with others who will hold your hand and offer shoulders and ears for support.

From: Mary Greer
To: Tina Greer
Cc: Liam Greer, Carl Morrison
Date: April 28, 2015 10:13 AM
Subject: Flowers

Tina and Carl,

The flowers arrived yesterday afternoon and they are beautiful. Thank you so much.

Michelle's service ended up being really nice. Malcolm did a music/photo montage of her life in better days that really helped us to focus on and recall the good times. What made it really special is that all of the songs were of her singing–back when she and Marc and Malcolm used to do music together. If I can figure out the technology, maybe I can show it to you when you are here this summer. She was truly talented. But it still sucks and she is much on my mind. Look forward to talking soon.

Love, Mary

From: Malcolm Charles
To: Marc Charles, Mary Greer
Date: July 28, 2015 9:51 AM
Subject: Re: Michelle on SC

Whoa, The Arrowheads have 18 followers! (All women, I think.) A few people have "favorited" a couple of our songs. (Eva, and Wonder.) A modest amount of listens, but still, this is pretty neat. Adding Mary. Mary, see the link below.
soundcloud.com/thearrowheads

From: Mary Greer
To: Malcolm Charles
Cc: Marc Charles
Date: July 28, 2015 11:41 AM
Subject: Re: Michelle on SC

Wow . . . how she would have loved this validation. Malcolm, thanks for doing this. I plan to listen to all of them later today, but wanted to respond quickly.
(Coincidentally, I dreamed about her last night. I dream about her a lot, actually. Not bad dreams–they tend to take the form of I can't find her, but then I do. Part of the grieving process, I guess.)

From: Malcolm Charles
To: Mary Greer, Marc Charles
Date: October 28, 2015 2:56 PM
Subject: article

From PBS

Sending because Mary, you mentioned I believe that Michelle had a dream like this just before she died, about Dad and her dogs, correct?

Love,
Malcolm

From: Marc Charles
To: Malcolm Charles
Cc: Mary Greer
Date: October 30, 2015 12:29 AM
Subject: Re: article

Wow, amazing research, and somewhat comforting too.

From: Mary Greer
To: Marc Charles
Cc: Malcolm Charles
Date: October 30, 2015 8:47 AM
Subject: Re: article

Malcolm,

Thanks so much for sending this. Yes, when I was visiting her at the nursing home, Michelle told me she had a very vivid dream about Dad and Wolfie. And similar to what the people say in this article, she specifically said the dream felt so real, and that it was a good dream. It is also interesting that she did not dream about Scooter, or you, or me, or anyone else who is alive. It makes you wonder if they were really there to help her cross over–I would really like to think that. (I hope I don't sound too much like a nutjob, and I am glad this is a PBS story, because it makes it seem less wacky.)

Love, Mary

From: Marc Charles
To: Mary Greer
Cc: Malcolm Charles
Date: October 30, 2015 10:30 PM
Subject: Re: article

That's a very nice thought - helping her cross over . . .

2016

From: Mary Greer
To: Marc Charles, Malcolm Charles
Date: January 7, 2016 11:11 AM
Subject: April 24

Marc and Malcolm,
Marc's email this morning prompted me to follow up about Michelle's ashes. Obviously, we didn't do anything this fall, and I really need to get this resolved. April 24 is a Sunday. By then, the canal will be spring-like and walkable. Could we get on everyone's calendars to meet that morning and go down there to do this? Malcolm, if you want to do anything else with a portion, that would give you time to set that up. Please let me know.

Also, I need to figure out what do with her car. My yard looks like one of those old "Men from Maine" jokes. Marc, did you ever talk to your attorney? Can I just have a junkman come and get it, so long as I don't take any money?

Love, Mary

From: Malcolm Charles
To: Mary Greer, Marc Charles
Date: January 7, 2016 3:26 PM
Subject: Re: April 24

A question: I'm wondering if you may be willing to consider this in February, though I concede that could be a tall order. I mention this because Peter will have both Monday and Tuesday off the week of President's Day, I may have to go overseas in March, and we're traveling for Peter's spring break the week of Easter Sunday.

I am not keen to travel in February, believe me, but since Peter's in school now, we don't want to have him absent for a family-enforced long weekend, plus we don't get to see each other, and the kids (my kids, anyway) don't get to see their cousins, I'd like to schedule this for a long weekend if possible. Of course, it could be like the Arctic that weekend, but it'd make this easier for the out-of-state family . . .

Let me know what you think, please.

Malcolm

From: Mary Greer
To: Malcolm Charles
Cc: Marc Charles
Date: January 7, 2016 7:08 PM
Subject: Re: April 24

February would be fine with me. Just keep in mind that if there is a lot of snow, the canal will be impassable–they don't plow or shovel or anything like that. We literally would not be able to get to that spot. But we probably could find somewhere on the canal to do it, and maybe there wouldn't be any snow anyway. So, I am game to go for it if you guys are.

It would also have to be on the Saturday or Sunday of President's Day weekend (either the 13th or 14th) because Jamie has to attend an "Accepted Students Overnight" thing at his college on that Monday and Tuesday, so he won't be home and I have to drop him off and pick him up on Monday/Tuesday. (We are really happy–he also got an 8K scholarship to boot!)

But Malcolm, (and Marc for that matter), if it is too much to travel up here, then just let it go. Marc and I can do it, and if it comes to it, I can actually do it myself. You already came to the service, so if you can't do the ashes, then don't worry about it. (Michelle herself didn't go to Dad's ashes thing.) I just really want to get this done–her ashes are here in my office and while it is not creepy or anything like that, it does weigh on me and it is time.

Anyway, let me know.

Mary

From: Marc Charles
To: Malcolm Charles
Cc: Mary Greer
Date: January 7, 2016 10:21 PM
Subject: Re: April 24

I'm fine with either February or April.

From: Marc Charles
To: Mary Greer
Date: January 8, 2016 9:58 AM
Subject: Re: April 24

That's great news about Jamie - I hope he really enjoys the college experience, wherever he lands. On Michelle's car, it's ok to turn it over to a junk company, but maybe we can discuss briefly with Christine when you visit next week. The key is that you can't hand or sign over the title (which I physically possess) because you have no legal standing, as we didn't probate her estate. So I just want to make sure a junk dealer doesn't show up and ask for it, thinking he's going to sell the car whole, because he can't. He instead has to sell it as parts only. And I want to make sure he doesn't try to persuade you to hand over the title with money, threats, etc. So let's discuss - I'm probably making it sound like a much bigger deal than it is.

From: Mary Greer
To: Marc Charles
Date: January 8, 2016 11:08 AM
Subject: Re: April 24

Ok, yes, let's talk about the car when I see you guys next week. And will wait until Malcolm rings in with a date for the ashes.

From: Malcolm Charles
To: Mary Greer, Marc Charles
Date: February 4, 2016 4:03 PM
Subject: Re: Michelle's memorial

Hi,

I can't come up for President's Day weekend, it will have to be in April. Sorry if this complicates any planning.

Thanks,
Malcolm

From: Marc Charles
To: Malcolm Charles
Cc: Mary Greer
Date: February 4, 2016 10:12 PM
Subject: Re: Michelle's memorial

Ok with me . . .

From: Mary Greer
To: Marc Charles
Cc: Malcolm Charles
Date: February 5, 2016 8:07 AM
Subject: Re: Michelle's memorial

Hi, guys,

That is totally fine with me, too. Can we set a firm date in April, though? April 24 is a Sunday. Will that work? Or the day before, Saturday, April 23?

Mary

From: Marc Charles
To: Mary Greer
Date: March 24, 2016 10:55 AM
Subject: Re: March-18

Sounds great! Do you happen to know how many miles are on Michelle's Saturn? It's a Vue, right?

From: Mary Greer
To: Marc Charles
Date: March 24, 2016 11:22 AM
Subject: Re: March-18

Yes, it is a 2006 Saturn Vue. On the mileage, right now the car is squished between our boat and the fence and I am quite seriously concerned about the boat falling on me when I open the car door. I did a brief look and I think you might have to start it, because I couldn't see anything on the dash. But I have her emissions report from March 2014 and it lists the odometer as 31,499. I know she hardly drove anywhere at all in the year before she died, so is that good enough? If not, let me know and I will have Liam try to start it when he gets home.

From: Marc Charles
To: Mary Greer
Date: March 24, 2016 11:41 AM
Subject: Re: March-18

Good enough for now - I'll keep you posted . . .

From: Marc Charles
To: Mary Greer
Date: March 28, 2016 10:11 AM
Subject: . . .

Mary - Did I by any chance mail the Saturn title to you a year ago when you were about to turn in the license plates? I really can't find it now.

From: Mary Greer
To: Marc Charles
Date: March 28, 2016 10:40 AM
Subject: Re: . . .

Oh, dear. No, in fact you specifically told me that you had it and that I didn't need it to turn in the plates (and you were right). All I have is a bunch of old registrations, emissions reports, and the plate return receipt.

From: Mary Greer
To: Marc Charles
Date: March 28, 2016 10:55 AM
Subject: Re: . . .

Marc,

Plumbing my memory, I vaguely recall you saying that you always had the title–you never actually gave it to Michelle even when it was paid off. You just held on to it for her. So, maybe it wouldn't have been with the more recent Michelle papers. Does that help? Would you have held onto the older stuff somewhere else?

Mary

From: Marc Charles
To: Malcolm Charles
Cc: Mary Greer
Date: November 10, 2016 5:14 PM
Subject: Re: Resending

I know Michelle kept throwing stuff away when she started moving from one address to another in 2004. As she downsized from the house to a condo to an apartment to a mobile home she had to keep getting rid of stuff. Liam and I found nothing that looked like a photo album when we took one last look at her stuff in the warehouse after she died.

2017

From: Mary Greer
To: Marc Charles
Date: March 15, 2017 12:44 PM
Subject: Landlord

Sigh . . . See link. I wonder if Michelle's trailer was one of the ones demo'ed.

From: Marc Charles
To: Mary Greer
Date: May 15, 2017 12:19 AM
Subject: Re: Landlord

I kind of hope it was, as it would mean he didn't make any money on a sale. But who knows? Easy enough to find out by just driving by it at some point. If I'm ever in the vicinity, I'll try to take a look. Hope all is well with the Greers.

2018

From: Mary Greer
To: Malcolm Charles, Marc Charles
Date: June 25, 2018 9:14 AM
Subject: Atlantic article

Interesting article from The Atlantic about the brain and alcoholism. It is certainly true that Mom and Michelle had an unusually low tolerance for stress and anxiety. But who knows? Anyway, in case you want to read it. I thought it was pretty interesting.

From: Marc Charles
To: Mary Greer
Cc: Malcolm Charles
Date: June 25, 2018 11:12 PM
Subject: Re: Atlantic article

Thanks Mary. Seems like a promising breakthrough; I really hope it leads to something good. It's the disease from hell.

2020

From: Mary Greer
To: Malcolm Charles, Marc Charles
Date: February 14, 2020 1:17 PM
Subject: Scooter

Just wanted to let you know that Michelle's dog, Scooter, passed away last night. He had a good long life—we think he was somewhere around 20 years old. He had a great time over the last five years with us (and especially with Rex, one of our other dogs), so I feel good about that. I hope he is with Michelle now. ☹

Love, Mary

EPILOGUE

2021

My sister died of cirrhosis at the age of 53. Five years after her death, I was looking for something related to her in my email, and did a search of her name. I began to read the emails from the earliest ones I had and realized they created a real-time narrative of the havoc caused by addiction. I compiled all my emails into this document. Note that this is only from MY email: no conversations; no interpretations from anyone else; things often open-ended with no resolution; there are holes in the narrative. Still, it is a window into the chaos of alcoholism.

Drinking not only caused my sister's life to be ruined (indeed, it ended it), but also had an enormous impact on her family. Strangely, there are no emails from her; I think perhaps by that point she no longer had a computer. The main character in this story has no voice. Yet we are all absorbed in her—constantly on edge waiting for the next disaster to strike.

I have done this compilation in the hope that it helps someone else to see the process of the addiction downward spiral, its impact on her family, and perhaps to identify what could have been done differently. It is unvarnished—we don't look great but we cared, we tried, and we loved her. We "did it wrong," but I am not sure anything would have been right. It also shows how difficult it really was to get any help. At various points, the system failed us.

Common, I think, to families impacted by addiction is that her siblings all argued and there were hard feelings among us, when it was really about her. I have changed all names and locations to protect her, and also to make it less a "true story" and more a universal tale. I did not change or delete anything embarrassing or that made any of us look bad.

Our mother was also an alcoholic who died in her early sixties. After living through the horror of that, my sister was a teetotaler until approximately her mid-thirties. At some point, probably related to the breakdown of her marriage, she began to drink and her decline was rapid. Our situation was especially difficult because she was a middle-aged adult by that time and so were we—we all had our own families and jobs.

It takes the entire compilation—through her résumé and the memorial—to get a true picture of what a tragedy this was, to cut through the anger and mess to realize how much talent was wasted. So much time has now passed that my hope is that our experience can help other families or be used to train addiction specialists.

My sister is at peace now. I dream about her still, and think about her every day.

Mary Greer

About the Author

Mary Greer, Ph.D. is one of the myriad people in the United States profoundly impacted by a family member's addiction to alcohol.

www.ingramcontent.com/pod-product-compliance
Lightning Source LLC
LaVergne TN
LVHW011834060526
838200LV00053B/4021